PENGUIN CLASSI

LETTERS TO A YOUNG

RAINER MARIA RILKE, one of the finest and most widely read poets of the twentieth century, was born in Prague in 1875. He published a great deal of verse early on, which is now little read, but with *The Book of Images* (1902), *The Book of Hours* (1905), and especially *New Poems* (1907 and 1908), he established himself as the major poet writing in German at the time. He married in 1901 and had a daughter, but abandoned family life almost immediately. In 1910 he published his only novel, *The Notebooks of Malte Laurids Brigge*, which draws in part on his own experiences of Paris, where he went in 1902 to write a short and brilliant book on Rodin (*Auguste Rodin*, 1903). Despite travelling widely, Paris was the main geographical pole in Rilke's life until the First World War, when he was stranded in Munich. From there, after the war, he moved to Switzerland, completing the *Duino Elegies* in 1922, which he had begun ten years before, and receiving the 'dictation' of the *Sonnets to Orpheus*. After this, while living in the French-speaking Valais, he wrote more in French than in German, and published *Vergers suivi des Quatrains Valaisans* a few months before his death from leukaemia at the end of 1926. After his death a lot of important uncollected poetry gradually emerged, as well as two further collections in French. The publication of his enormous correspondence, still not complete, began with the appearance of *Letters to a Young Poet* in 1929.

CHARLIE LOUTH was born in Bristol in 1969. He is a Fellow of The Queen's College, Oxford, where he lectures in German. His translations of Friedrich Hölderlin's *Essays and Letters* (with Jeremy Adler) appeared in Penguin Classics in 2009.

LEWIS HYDE is a poet, essayist, translator and cultural critic with a particular interest in the public life of the imagination. His books include *The Gift* (1993), *Trickster Makes This World* (1998) and *Common as Air* (2010). The former director of undergraduate creative writing at Harvard University, Hyde teaches during the fall semester at Kenyon College, where he is the Richard L. Thomas Professor of Creative Writing. During the rest of the year he lives in Cambridge, Massachusetts, where he is a Faculty Associate at Harvard's Berkman Center for Internet and Society.

RAINER MARIA RILKE

Letters to a Young Poet
&
The Letter from the
Young Worker

*Translated, Edited and with Notes and
an Afterword by* CHARLIE LOUTH

Introduction by LEWIS HYDE

PENGUIN BOOKS

PENGUIN CLASSICS

Published by the Penguin Group
Penguin Books Ltd, 80 Strand, London WC2R ORL, England
Penguin Group (USA) Inc., 375 Hudson Street, New York, New York 10014, USA
Penguin Group (Canada), 90 Eglinton Avenue East, Suite 700, Toronto, Ontario,
Canada M4P 2Y3 (a division of Pearson Penguin Canada Inc.)
Penguin Ireland, 25 St Stephen's Green, Dublin 2, Ireland (a division of Penguin Books Ltd)
Penguin Group (Australia), 707 Collins Street, Melbourne, Victoria 3008, Australia
(a division of Pearson Australia Group Pty Ltd)
Penguin Books India Pvt Ltd, 11 Community Centre, Panchsheel Park,
New Delhi – 110 017, India
Penguin Group (NZ), 67 Apollo Drive, Rosedale, Auckland 0632, New Zealand
(a division of Pearson New Zealand Ltd)
Penguin Books (South Africa) (Pty) Ltd, Block D, Rosebank Office Park, 181 Jan Smuts Avenue,
Parktown North, Gauteng 2193, South Africa

Penguin Books Ltd, Registered Offices: 80 Strand, London WC2R ORL, England

www.penguin.com

This translation first published in Penguin Books (UK) 2011
Published in Penguin Books (USA) 2013

032

Copyright Insel Verlag Frankfurt am Main, 1929, 1933
Translation, afterword, chronology and notes copyright © Charlie Louth, 2011
Introduction copyright © Lewis Hyde, 2011

This English-language edition of *Briefe an einen jungen Dichter* and *Der Brief des jungen Arbeiters*
published by arrangement with Insel Verlag Berlin.

Set in Postscript Adobe Sabon
Typeset by Ellipsis Books Limited
Printed and bound in Great Britain by Clays Ltd, Elcograf S.p.A.

ISBN: 978-0-141-19232-1

www.greenpenguin.co.uk

Contents

Chronology

1875 4 *December* Rilke born prematurely in Prague and christened René Karl Wilhelm Johann Josef Maria. His parents belong to the German-speaking minority in Bohemia, part of the Austro-Hungarian Empire.

1882 Rilke's education begins at a school run by Piarists.

1884 His parents, Josef and Sophie (Phia), move into separate flats.

1886 Enters the Military Lower School at St Pölten in Lower Austria.

1890 Moves up to the Military Academy in Mährisch-Weisskirchen (present-day Hranice), a school also attended a few years later by the novelist Robert Musil. By now Rilke is writing poems.

1891 Poorly and unhappy in Mährisch-Weisskirchen, Rilke quits and moves to the Academy for Trade and Commerce in Linz. *September* Publishes his first poem. Reading Tolstoy.

1892 Leaves the Linz Academy without qualification and returns to Prague to study privately for his Matura (school-leaving certificate). Reading Goethe.

1894 *November* Publication of his first collection of poems, *Leben und Lieder* (*Lives and Songs*), which he later disowned.

1895 Having gained his Matura in July (with distinction), matriculates at the University of Prague, attending lectures on art history, literature and philosophy. Busy in the literary world, and writing plays and prose as well as poems. *Larenopfer* (*Offerings to the Lares*) appears just before Christmas.

1896 *September* Quits Prague for Munich, where he studies art history. *December* Publishes *Traumgekrönt* (*Crowned with Dreams*).

1897 *May* Meets and pursues Lou Andreas-Salomé, and in June withdraws with her to a country retreat outside Munich. Transforms his handwriting, and at her suggestion adopts the name Rainer. Over the next year writes a collection of poems to her, *Dir zur Feier* (*To Celebrate You*), which is never published. *October* Moves to Berlin and takes lodgings near Andreas-Salomé and her husband. Attends a reading by Stefan George in November and publishes *Advent* in time for Christmas.

1898 *March* Returns to Prague to give a well-attended lecture on 'Modern Poetry'. Publishes the first of several volumes of stories. While in Florence keeps the so-called 'Florentine Diary' (published 1942). Back in Berlin with Andreas-Salomé, then spends Christmas with Heinrich Vogeler in Bremen and Worpswede.

1899 *April–June* Journey to Russia, in the company of the Andreas couple. Visits Tolstoy and meets the painter Leonid Pasternak. Publishes *Mir zur Feier* (*To Celebrate Myself*) at the end of the year.

1900 *May–August* More travels in Russia, alone with Andreas-Salomé. This journey was preceded by an intensive study of things Russian, including the translation of Chekhov's *Seagull*. At the end of August accepts an invi-

tation from Vogeler to Worpswede, where he meets Clara
Westhoff and Paula Becker. *October* Returns to Berlin.

1901 *February* Lou Andreas-Salomé breaks off relationship
with Rilke by letter. *28 April* He marries Clara Westhoff.
They set up home in Westerwede, where a daughter,
Ruth, is born on 12 December.

1902 In need of money, undertakes to write a monograph
on the Worpswede artists. Also reviewing widely. In July
Das Buch der Bilder (*The Book of Images*) appears
(poems). *August* Goes to Paris with a commission for a
book on Rodin, leaving his daughter with Clara's par-
ents. Probably in November, writes 'The Panther', the
first of what will become the *New Poems*. The book on
Rodin is written by the end of the year.

1903 First letter to Franz Xaver Kappus written on 17
February. Publishes *Worpswede* (February) and *Auguste
Rodin* (March). Travels, but is mostly in Paris until
September when with Clara he goes to Rome. Exchanges
important letters with Lou Andreas-Salomé.

1904 In Rome until June, then to Sweden via Denmark.
Begins work on his novel, *The Notebooks of Malte
Laurids Brigge*. All but one of the *Letters to a Young
Poet* are written by the end of this year.

1905 Mostly in Germany until September when he moves
into Rodin's house in Meudon, outside Paris. He works
as a kind of secretary, dealing with Rodin's correspond-
ence. *Das Stunden-Buch* (*The Book of Hours*) appears
at the end of the year, beginning Rilke's association with
the Insel Press. Its three parts had been written in 1899,
1901 and 1903.

1906 Lectures on Rodin in Hamburg and Berlin. *March*
His father dies. After a misunderstanding with Rodin,

moves into his own lodgings in Paris. Working hard on the *New Poems*. In the summer travels in Belgium; then in Germany and Italy, ending up on Capri in December. Second, much-revised edition of *The Book of Images* appears. Also *Die Weise von Liebe und Tod des Cornets Christoph Rilke* (*The Lay of the Love and Death of the Cornet Christoph Rilke*) in book form.

1907 Remains in Capri until the end of May. With the help of his host, Alice Faehndrich, translates Elizabeth Barrett Browning's *Sonnets from the Portuguese* (published 1908). Returns to Paris. Frequent visits to Cézanne retrospective exhibition on which he writes a famous series of letters to Clara (published in 1952). *August* Writes nearly half the poems that will appear in the second volume of *New Poems*. *December* The first, *Neue Gedichte*, is published.

1908 Capri, Rome, Paris. *Der Neuen Gedichte anderer Teil* (*Second Part of the New Poems*). *December* Last letter to Franz Xaver Kappus.

1909 Working on his novel in Paris. Twice in Provence, impressions of which (especially Avignon) go much later into *The Letter from the Young Worker*. Publishes *Requiem*, two elegies, of which one is for Paula Modersohn-Becker who died in childbirth late in 1907.

1910 The final pages of *Die Aufzeichnungen des Malte Laurids Brigge* (*The Notebooks of Malte Laurids Brigge*) dictated in Leipzig; *May* The novel appears. This is followed by an unsettled period – travels in Italy, Bohemia, Austria, Germany, and, embarking in Marseille, Algeria and Tunisia, Sicily and Naples.

1911 The journey continues to Egypt and up the Nile. *April* Back to Paris via Venice. Visits Aristide Maillol. Meets

Marthe Hennebert, probably the 'Marthe' of *The Letter from the Young Worker*. Reading St Augustine, and translates first eighteen chapters of the *Confessions*; many other bits of translation besides. *July* In Prague for the last time. Then Weimar, Leipzig, Munich. From late October in Castle of Duino on the Adriatic coast, as the guest of Marie von Thurn und Taxis.

1912 While in Duino, where he remains until May, writes first two of what will become the *Duino Elegies*, plus other fragments. Spends the summer in Venice, then autumn and winter in Spain, mainly Toledo and Ronda.

1913 *February* Back in Paris. Travels in Germany in the summer, then in September is in Munich where he meets Freud, in the company of Andreas-Salomé. *October* Returns to Paris. Reading Expressionist poets and Kleist. Finishes the third Elegy. Publishes *Das Marien-Leben* (*Life of Mary*), a sequence of thirteen poems.

1914 Paris remains his base until July. Reading Hölderlin. Is caught in Munich by the outbreak of war and cannot return to Paris. *December* In Berlin.

1915 Reading Hölderlin, Strindberg, Montaigne, Flaubert, the Bible, Kierkegaard. *April* His belongings in Paris are auctioned to cover the unpaid rent. Writes 'Seven Poems' and the fourth Elegy. *24 November* Rilke is called up. Efforts to avoid this delay things until the end of the year.

1916 Reports for training at a barracks in Vienna but is soon transferred to the Imperial War Archives, where Stefan Zweig is also employed. *June* Discharged and returns to Munich in July. *27 November* Death in a rail accident of Rilke's friend Emile Verhaeren, the Belgian poet to whom *The Letter from the Young Worker* is addressed. Gathers together but does not publish a group of poems under the title 'Gedichte an die Nacht' ('Poems to the Night').

1917 Translating Michelangelo's sonnets. In Munich until July, then Berlin, Westphalia, Berlin (where he learns of the death of Rodin in November), and back in Munich in December where he lives in the Hotel Continental until the following May. Publishes *Die vierundzwanzig Sonette der Louize Labé* (*The Twenty-Four Sonnets of Louise Labé*) (translations).

1918 Does not leave Munich but in May moves into lodgings. One of his neighbours is Paul Klee. Continues work on Michelangelo. Sends copies of his 'Elegies' (roughly half of what will become the *Duino Elegies*) to Lou Andreas-Salomé and to his publisher for safe keeping. Follows the events of the November Revolution in Munich closely, taking part in demonstrations and associating with some of the revolutionaries, such as Ernst Toller.

1919 As well as Michelangelo, translates poems by Verhaeren and Mallarmé. Is shaken by the assassination of the socialist Kurt Eisner, the first minister-president of the Free State of Bavaria. As part of the counter-revolution Rilke's flat is twice searched. *May* Lou Andreas-Salomé in Munich, their last meeting. *11 June* Leaves Germany for Switzerland with a ten-day permit, never to return. Begins a reading tour in late October. From December is in Locarno.

1920 Having been issued with a Czech passport, travels to Venice in June/July and to Paris in October. Otherwise restlessly in Switzerland, from November in Berg am Irchel. Begins relationship with Baladine Klossowska.

1921 Translating Paul Valéry. After much searching for an 'elegy-place', moves into the Château de Muzot in the Valais at the end of July.

1922 *February* Completes the *Duino Elegies*; also *The Sonnets to Orpheus* and *The Letter from the Young Worker*. Continues to translate Valéry. Reading Proust.

1923 Early symptoms of illness. Publication of *Die Sonette an Orpheus* (March) and *Duineser Elegien* (October). Critical of political developments in Germany. Makes small trips within Switzerland. At the end of the year enters the sanatorium in Valmont.

1924 20 *January* Returns to Muzot. Begins writing many poems in French. Among flow of other visitors receives Valéry, whose works he continues to translate. In Ragaz in the summer. Autumn in Bern and then the sanatorium in Valmont.

1925 *January–August* In Paris. Recovers two boxes of letters and papers not auctioned in 1915. Works with Maurice Betz on translation of *Malte* into French. *September* Two weeks in Ragaz, then back in Muzot. Makes his will. *November* Translation of Valéry's poems appears. Regrets not being able to read Lawrence and Joyce in the original. In Valmont again before Christmas.

1926 In the sanatorium until the end of May. *Vergers suivi des Quatrains Valaisans* appears in Paris – this collection of Rilke's poems in French is followed by *Les Roses* and *Les Fenêtres* in 1927. Three-way correspondence with Marina Tsvetaeva and Boris Pasternak. *June* Sends a selection of unpublished German poems to the Insel Press. Summer in Ragaz, then Lausanne. Back in the Valais, translates Valéry's dialogues *Eupalinos* and

L'Âme et la danse. *30 November* Taken to Valmont in great pain. Finally diagnosed with leukaemia. *29 December* Dies.

1929 *Briefe an einen jungen Dichter* (*Letters to a Young Poet*) published, as a first sample of Rilke's correspondence.

1933 *Der Brief des jungen Arbeiters* (*The Letter from the Young Worker*) published in *Über Gott: Zwei Briefe* (*On God: Two Letters*).

Charlie Louth 2011

Introduction

A GEOGRAPHY OF SOLITUDE

Letters to a Young Poet could as easily have been called
Letters from a Young Poet. Rainer Maria Rilke was only
twenty-six years old when Franz Xaver Kappus first wrote
to him in 1902. As the addresses on Rilke's letters indi-
cate, he had no settled home (first he's in Paris, then on
the Italian coast, then at an art colony in northern
Germany, then in Rome, then in Sweden, then back in
Paris). Three years before these letters start, he had mar-
ried the sculptor Clara Westhoff and fathered a child, but
he and his wife rarely lived together, nor did they raise
their daughter (they left that task to Clara's parents).
Nonetheless, he was not without a sense of family obliga-
tion. 'The last two years since my marriage I really have
tried to earn, continually, day by day,' he wrote to a friend
in the same week as the second letter to Kappus, confess-
ing that 'not much has come of it' and that it left him
feeling 'as if someone had closed the window towards the
garden in which my songs live'.

As for those songs, Rilke had clearly dedicated himself
to poetry and had been publishing since the early 1890s,
but he could not yet be sure that the work would give

him sufficient foundation in the world. The letter just cited continues: 'I have written eleven or twelve books and have received almost nothing for them ...' Some years earlier he had enrolled himself in a business school (an experiment that lasted only a few months), and he periodically dreamed that he might become a schoolteacher or a doctor or more simply 'seek rescue in some quiet handicraft'.

Nor was Rilke entirely free of his parents. Concurrent with the letters he sent to Kappus are letters sent to him by his father, letters in which Josef Rilke expressed concern that his son had failed to find a respectable career and offered to secure him a civil service job in Prague. Just before a visit to his parents in August of 1903, his father wrote to worry about the way that Rilke dressed and to suggest that he order himself a new suit. In those days when Rilke fell to musing on his ideal poetic career he would find his reveries interrupted by the word 'imprudent' spoken in his father's voice.

As for Rilke's mother, she visited him in Rome a month before the seventh letter to Kappus. 'Every meeting with her is a kind of setback,' he wrote to a friend.

When I have to see this lost, unreal woman who is connected with nothing, who cannot grow old, I feel how even as a child I struggled to get away from her and fear deep within me lest after years and years of running and walking I am still not far enough from her, that somewhere inwardly I still make movements that are the other half of her embittered gestures ... Then I have a horror of her distraught pieties ... herself empty as a dress, ghostly and terrible. And that still I am her child; that some

scarcely recognizable wallpaper door in this faded wall
that doesn't belong to anything was my entrance into the
world ... !

The sympathetic intelligence described here, the kind that
leads a man 'inwardly' to complete someone else's gestures,
is a part of Rilke's poetic genius to be sure (how else could
he have written the remarkable poem about the panther
in the Paris zoo?). At the same time, this ability to identify
with others sometimes led Rilke to lose his own bearings.
In August 1902, about six months before these letters
begin, Rilke had travelled to Paris to write a monograph
on the sculptor Auguste Rodin. The trip was a turning
point in his life: the older man offered a model of how an
artist can ground himself in steady, patient work. Nonethe-
less, Rilke hated Paris. He felt invisible and alone,
surrounded by men and women driven like machines,
people 'holding out under the foot of each day that trod
on them, like tough beetles'. Their 'burdened lives', he told
a friend, threatened to swamp him:

> I often had to say aloud to myself that I was not one of
> them ... And yet, when I noticed how my clothes were
> becoming worse and heavier from week to week ... I was
> frightened and felt that I would belong irretrievably to the
> lost if some passer-by merely looked at me and half uncon-
> sciously counted me with them.

In great detail he described the morning when he came
upon a man suffering from the nervous disease known as
St Vitus's Dance. It is hardly an exaggeration to say that
Rilke was possessed by what he saw:

No one paid any attention to him; but I, who couldn't keep my eyes off him even for a second, knew how gradually the restlessness was returning, how it became stronger and stronger ... how it shook at his shoulders, how it clung to his head to tear it out of balance, and how suddenly it quite unexpectedly overcame and broke up his walk.

Feeling 'will-less', Rilke followed the man whose fears, he felt, were 'no longer distinguishable from mine'. Finally he broke away and returned to his rooms, 'exhausted', used up by someone else's malady. He had been on his way to the library but the trip now seemed pointless; there couldn't possibly be a book powerful enough to expel the thing that had taken hold of him.

In sketching this background to the 'young poet' letters, I have been quoting from Rilke's concurrent correspondence with more intimate acquaintances. In the Kappus letters, Rilke sometimes hints at his own difficulties (as when he says that his 'life is full of troubles and sadness') but, as might be expected, he never lays them out in any detail. The letters to friends are less reticent, however, and one of their surprises is how often Rilke speaks of being anxious and afraid. Afraid of what? Afraid, I think, that he might never become his own person. In the seventh letter to Kappus, Rilke mentions the way in which most people, faced with the difficulties of sexual love, 'escape into one of the many conventions which like public shelters are set up ... along this most dangerous of paths'. Clearly, Rilke himself did not wish to take shelter, but the temptation was obviously there – to settle down, to support his wife and child, to buy himself a good suit, to follow a path that no one could call imprudent. As with many young artists, Rilke had a sense of the land to which his gifts might lead him, but he was also anxious that he might never get there. He lived in fear of two false fates: either that he might end up as lost as the ragged poor who had surrounded him in Paris or else that he might succumb to the safe but numbing comforts of convention.

It is in these terms that I understand one of the great themes laid out in the letters collected here, the idea that poetic practice requires solitude. In the vision Rilke offers, solitude is not merely a matter of being alone: it is a territory to be entered and occupied, and Rilke provides for Kappus (and the rest of us) a map of how to accomplish those ends. The first step is the simple recognition that solitude exists. A lack of connection to other people, after all, is not something we are normally eager to seek, acknowledge or welcome. Rilke himself hardly assented to the isolation he felt during his schooling in military academies ('when I was a boy among boys, I was alone among them'), nor did he welcome it when he moved to Paris to write about Rodin ('how alone I was this time among these people, how perpetually disowned by all I met'). In both cases, gloom and fear had overcome him. In Paris, before going to bed at night he used to read the Book of Job for solace: 'It was all true of me, word for word!'

Compare that touch of self-pity with the advice to Kappus: 'We *are* solitary. It is possible to deceive yourself and act as if it were not the case ... How much better ... to take it as our starting-point.' I don't at all mean to imply by this juxtaposition that Rilke is being hypocritical. I mean, instead, to point to the spiritual intelligence that led him to convert solitude from a curse into a blessing.

Rather than continue to suffer under his sense of aloneness, Rilke eventually did what he urges Kappus to do: he turned and embraced it. He took isolation to be a given, then entered and inhabited it.

This trick of reversal, of turning negatives into positives, became a regular part of Rilke's working method. Anxiety, fear, sadness, doubt: there is no human emotion that cannot be upended and put into service. Anxiety, he tells Kappus, should be thought of as 'existential anxiety', the kind that God requires of us in order to begin. The desire to flee from solitude can be converted into 'a kind of tool' to make solitude still larger. When doubts arise, simply '*school* them': 'instead of being demolishers they will be among your best workers'.

To enter willingly the land of solitude does not, of course, mean that what follows will be easy. In my own experience, embracing solitude brings on another order of difficulties. When I was young and beginning to write, I used to put myself through periods of ritual retreat. I would cut off the telephone and the mail, unplug the television and the radio, take a short-term vow of silence, pull down the window shades and settle in to work for three or four days. Often on the first day, much to my chagrin, I would fall into a depression. The whole exercise suddenly seemed pointless; I had my pen in my hand but nothing to say.

Something similar used to happen to Rilke. To take a key example, Rilke was living more or less alone in a medieval castle on the Adriatic coast near Trieste when, in the winter of 1911–12, he began to write the *Duino Elegies*. As the owner of the estate, Marie Taxis, reported, the retreat started badly: 'A great sadness befell him, and he began to suspect that this winter would … fail to produce anything.' As Rilke himself told his patron: 'Things must first get bad, worse, worst, beyond what any language can hold. I creep about all day in the thickets of my life, screaming like a wild man and clapping my hands. You would not believe what hair-raising creatures this flushes up.'

It is worth pausing over the mention of 'sadness', both because 'great sadnesses' figure in the letters to Kappus and because they belong to the geography of solitude. Solitude was for Rilke the necessary enclosure within which he could begin to form an independent identity, a sense of himself free from the callings of family and convention. Solitude is the alembic of personhood, as the alchemists might have said. And yet its entrances seem to be guarded by feelings that would make most people turn and walk the other way – not just sadness, but anxiety, fear, doubt, premonitions of death, 'all unsettling, all pain, all depression of spirit ...'

Rilke's simple suggestion is that the discipline of art demands a turning towards, rather than away from, such states of mind. They portend necessary labours and must thus be taken seriously. He asks Kappus to imagine that sadness indicates a moment 'when something new enters into us' and that we then have duties towards the unfamiliar thing. It may in fact be fate itself, a destiny which, with proper attention, we can absorb and make our own. 'We have no reason to be mistrustful of our world ... If it holds terrors they are *our* terrors' and we should try to love them. They are like the dragons in old myth that, when approached directly, turn out not to be dragons at all but helpless royalty in need of our attentions.

Whatever the exact metaphysics of such encounters, the point is that an exploration of the land of solitude cannot begin until we have accepted solitude as a fact ('We *are* alone!') and then faced the minatory moods that stand just inside its gates. And what happens after that? If acceptance comes and sadness is endured, what follows?

What follows is a change of consciousness in regard particularly to time. The very first of Rilke's letters to Kappus distinguishes between life's 'most inconsequential and slightest hour' and the clearly more desirable 'quietest hour' of the night. This latter is not, I think, an hour at all. It has no knowable dimension. 'All distances, all measurements, alter for the one who becomes solitary', especially the measurement of time: 'a year has no meaning, and ten years are nothing. To be an artist means: not to calculate and count; to grow and ripen like a tree ...' Creative life contains its own temporality and the surest way to make it fail is to put it on an external clock. Mechanical time makes haste, as it were, but haste dissolves in solitude. In solitude we feel 'as if eternity lay before' us.

Solitude can also mute the voice of judgement. Kappus included some poems in his first letter and he asked Rilke's opinion of them. Rilke offered one (the poems 'have no identity of their own') but then set out to interrogate evaluation itself: by what measure do we reckon a poem worthy or unworthy? Not by any measure that the outer world has to offer. Only one rule applies: 'A work of art is good if it has arisen out of necessity.' And how might a poet recognize this 'necessity'? Only by making the 'descent into yourself and into your solitariness'. In that isolated space, the world's criteria drop away. When Rilke writes in the third letter that 'an artist ... must always remain innocent and unconscious of his greatest virtues', I understand him to mean that questions of good and bad, virtue and vice, are foreign to the absorption of solitary work. As Flannery O'Connor once wrote: 'In art the self becomes self-forgetful in order to meet the demands of the thing seen and the thing being made.' Such has certainly been my own experience; in solitude (after a few days) the mind that weighs the work withdraws and I simply enter my material on its own terms. I may later find that what I have written is junk or that it is gold, but such labels have little currency in the confines of solitude.

After all this has unfolded – after acceptance has arrived, after doubts have become helpers, after evaluation has quietened down and time has opened up – then what happens?

Then nothing happens. Or, rather, then begins the practice of patience, a virtue in which Rilke had been schooled by Rodin. Rilke eventually published a book about Rodin and there he makes it clear that endurance was a necessary part of the older man's talent: 'There is in Rodin a deep patience which makes him almost anonymous, a quiet, wise forbearance, something of the great patience and kindness of Nature herself, who … traverses silently and seriously the long pathway to abundance.' In a letter to Rodin himself, written just after the final letter to Kappus, Rilke spelled out one moral of the master's 'tenacious example': 'ordinary life … seems to bid us haste', but patience 'puts us in touch with all that surpasses us'. Practised in the present, patience is the art of courting the future. It belongs to becoming rather than being, to the unfinished rather than the completed. It is not so much suited to heroes as to invalids and convalescents, those who must wait.

The flowering of any creative 'summer' will come, Rilke tells Kappus, 'only to those who are patient, who are simply there in their vast, quiet tranquillity, as if eternity lay before them. It is a lesson I learn every day … : *patience* is all!' Patience means sitting with the work even when – especially when – nothing appears to be happening.

The situation in which Rilke wrote the first *Duino Elegy* is again instructive. Marie Taxis later told the story: 'One morning he received a tedious business letter. Wishing to deal with it right away, he had to sit down and devote himself to figures and other dry matters. Outside a strong bora was blowing …' Descending from the castle to the bastions overlooking the sea, 'Rilke walked back and forth deep in thought, preoccupied with his answer to the letter. Then all at once … it seemed to him as though in the roar of the wind a voice had called out to him: "If I cried out, who could hear me up there among the angelic orders?"'

Having received the first line, Rilke set to work and, by nightfall, the first elegy was on paper. 'The *Duino Elegies* were not written,' observes William Gass, 'they were awaited.' Awaited in patience of course, though in this case patience had a curious added detail, that 'tedious business letter'. Should we count such annoyances as belonging to the geography of solitude? I think so. They are the distractions that force attention to wander, the catalysts of not-doing. All art requires effort but effort alone does not make the work, and distractions (so long as they are contained in solitude) are therefore useful. They are like the palladium atom that lets the carbon atoms bond, never itself becoming part of the new compound. That tedious business letter does not appear in the *Duino Elegies*, but there might be no elegies without it.

Here it should be said that Rilke never tells Kappus that a poet might find distraction useful. The letters to Kappus paint a grand portrait of how a poet works, and it will be worth pausing to interrogate that grandeur. I myself have often been put off by the extremity of Rilke's language. His modifiers are consistently superlatives: there is no deep but the deepest, no quiet but the quietest. Works of art are not just solitary but 'infinitely' so. Rodin did not only teach art but art's 'profundity and eternity'. References to 'purity' abound: irony ought to be 'used purely', feelings ought to be 'pure', sexuality ought to be 'entirely mature and pure'.

There is not much space in Rilke's vision for many of the things that were to happen later in twentieth-century art – for composition practices that rely on chance, for example, or the writing of what Pablo Neruda called 'impure poetry' (poetry 'corroded as if by acids, steeped in sweat and smoke, reeking of urine ...'). No, in Rilke we find 'fate' or 'destiny' rather than chance, and the desired ends are all of them highly refined. Approaching his elevated language a century after these letters were written, it is hard to resist offering a psychoanalytic reading. Surely what we have here is not just grandeur but grandiosity, the mind's reflexive response to the fear and anxiety that Rilke so clearly felt.

As plausible as that reading may be, however, it is worth asking if there isn't a way to approach Rilke's extremities on terms that he himself might recognize. In puzzling over that question I have found it helpful to think of words like 'purity', 'infinity' and 'eternity' as placeholders pointing towards all that does not yet exist, but might. They are abstractions of the kind that allow the mind to work with the unknown and the not-yet-real. They correspond to things like surds, irrational numbers and infinitesimals in mathematics, that is to say, to 'numbers' that cannot be expressed in ordinary, finite terms. Albert Einstein once wrote that 'as far as the laws of mathematics refer to reality, they are not certain; as far as they are certain, they do not refer to reality.' No one would say that mathematicians who work with surds or with the kind of axioms Einstein called 'free creations of the human mind' are involved in grandiose responses to their own neuroses. No, they are just doing mathematics. Nor are their unreal placeholders entirely divorced from real experience. Most of modern technology, from suspension bridges to airplanes, would not exist if Newton and Leibnitz had not entertained the idea of infinitesimals.

Let us suppose that the pure, unreal elements of Rilke's world perform a similar function, albeit in this case a spiritual or aesthetic one. In a 1903 letter, he wrote that an art object must be 'withdrawn from all chance ... lifted out of time and given to space ...' where it will become 'lasting, capable of eternity'. I cannot be sure what 'eternity' means here, but at the same time I cannot be sure that it has no meaning. In *The Letter from the Young Worker*, included at the end of this volume, the character Rilke has created recalls the iconography of the old churches: 'Here is the angel, who does not exist, and the devil, who does not exist; and man, who does exist, is in between them and ... their unreality makes him more real for me.' Here on earth it may be hard to find some of the things that Rilke mentions in the letters to Kappus – 'an infinitely tender hand', for example, or an 'infinitely solitary' work of art – but that does not mean the phrases have no function. Perhaps they lead us towards the outer edges of finite hands and finite works of art and, from there, towards imagining what lies beyond, what has not yet come to be. As the Young Worker says:

> Isn't our relationship to all the great unknown forces exactly like this? We experience none of them in their purity ... But isn't it the case with all scholars, explorers and inventors that the assumption that they were dealing with great forces suddenly led to the greatest of all?

In the letters that Rilke wrote to his friends and family during the years that he was writing to Kappus, he rarely mentions that parallel correspondence. An interesting exception is a letter of July 1904 to his wife Clara. She has forwarded one of Kappus's letters and Rilke remarks that the younger man 'is having a hard time', that he complains of having used up his strength. Rilke then, in a typical inversion, remarks that 'the using up of strength is in a certain sense still an increase of strength ...: all the strength we give away comes back over us again, experienced and transformed. Thus it is in prayer. And what is there that, truly done, would not be prayer?'

Rilke is speaking of Kappus's struggles of course, but he could as easily be speaking of his own. After all, in the letters to Kappus he offers up the strength he himself had by then acquired, and gives it away such that it might come back transformed. Of note, then, is the way his thoughts turn from donation to prayer, as if to say that a letter, 'truly done', is itself a form of invocation. That, in any event, is how I have come to understand the otherwise exaggerated language of these letters. It is surely the case that, from Kappus's position, the letters are hortatory and sermonizing. But to the degree that Rilke is speaking of and to himself – rehearsing his own trials in regard to poetry, family, sexuality, fear – the letters to a young poet are his prayers.

Lewis Hyde 2011

LETTERS TO A
YOUNG POET

Preface

In late autumn 1902 it was – I was sitting under ancient chestnut trees in the gardens of the Military Academy in Wiener Neustadt with a book. I was so absorbed by my reading that I hardly noticed it when the only one of our teachers who was not an army officer, Horaček, the learned and good-natured chaplain of the Academy, came and joined me. He took the volume from my hand, looked at the cover and shook his head. 'Poems by Rainer Maria Rilke?' he asked thoughtfully. He leafed through its pages, ran his eyes over a few verses, looked reflectively into the distance and finally nodded. 'So, our pupil René Rilke has become a poet.'

And I was told about the slight, pale boy sent by his parents more than fifteen years before to the Military Lower School in Sankt Pölten so that he might later become an officer. In those days Horaček had worked there as the chaplain and he still remembered his former pupil well. He described him as a quiet, serious, highly gifted child, who liked to keep himself to himself, put up with the discipline of boarding-school life patiently and after the fourth year moved on with the others to the Military Upper School in Mährisch-Weisskirchen. There his constitution proved not to be resilient enough, and so

*his parents took him out of the establishment and had him
continue his studies at home in Prague. What path his
career had taken after that Horaček was unable to say.*

*Given all this it is probably not difficult to understand
that I decided that very hour to send my poetic efforts to
Rainer Maria Rilke and ask him for his verdict. Not yet
twenty years old and on the verge of going into a profes-
sion which I felt was directly opposed to my true
inclinations, I thought that if anyone was going to under-
stand my situation it was the author of the book* To
Celebrate Myself. *And without its being my express inten-
tion, my verses were accompanied by a letter in which I
revealed myself more unreservedly than to anyone ever
before, or to anyone since.*

*Many weeks went by before an answer came. The letter
with its blue seal bore a Paris postmark, weighed heavy in
the hand and displayed on the envelope the same clarity,
beauty and assurance of hand with which the content itself
was written from the first line to the last. And so my regu-
lar correspondence with Rainer Maria Rilke began, lasting
until 1908 and then gradually petering out because life
forced me into domains which the poet's warm, tender and
moving concern had precisely wanted to protect me from.*

*But that is unimportant. The only important thing is the
ten letters that follow, important for the insight they give
into the world in which Rainer Maria Rilke lived and worked,
and important too for many people engaged in growth and
change, today and in the future. And where a great and
unique person speaks, the rest of us should be silent.*

*Franz Xaver Kappus
Berlin, June 1929*

Dear Sir,

Your letter only reached me a few days ago. Let me thank you for the great and endearing trust it shows. There is little more I can do. I cannot go into the nature of your verses, for any critical intention is too remote from me. There is nothing less apt to touch a work of art than critical words: all we end up with there is more or less felicitous misunderstandings. Things are not all as graspable and sayable as on the whole we are led to believe; most events are unsayable, occur in a space that no word has ever penetrated, and most unsayable of all are works of art, mysterious existences whose life endures alongside ours, which passes away.

Having begun with this preliminary remark, all I will go on to say is that your verses have no identity of their own, though they do have tacit and concealed hints of something personal. I feel that most clearly in the last poem, 'My Soul'. There something individual is trying to come into words, to find its manner. And in the lovely poem 'To Leopardi' perhaps a kind of affinity with this great and solitary man develops. Still, the poems are not yet anything in themselves, nothing self-sufficient, not even the last one and the one to Leopardi. The kind letter you wrote accompanying them does not fail to make many of the shortcomings I sensed in reading your verses explicable, without for all that being able to give them a name.

You ask whether your verses are good. You ask me that. You have asked others, before. You send them to magazines. You compare them with other poems, and you worry when certain editors turn your efforts down. Now (since you have allowed me to offer you advice) let me ask you to give up all that. You are looking to the outside, and that above all you should not be doing now. Nobody can advise you and help you, nobody. There is only one way. Go into yourself. Examine the reason that bids you to write; check whether it reaches its roots into the deepest region of your heart, admit to yourself whether you would die if it should be denied you to write. This above all: ask yourself in your night's quietest hour: *must* I write? Dig down into yourself for a deep answer. And if it should be affirmative, if it is given to you to respond to this serious question with a loud and simple '*I must*', then construct your life according to this necessity; your life right into its most inconsequential and slightest hour must become a sign and witness of this urge. Then approach nature. Then try, like the first human being, to say what you see and experience and love and lose. Don't write love poems; avoid at first those forms which are too familiar and habitual: they are the hardest, for you need great maturity and strength to produce something of your own in a domain where good and sometimes brilliant examples have been handed down to us in abundance. For this reason, flee general subjects and take refuge in those offered by your own day-to-day life; depict your sadnesses and desires, passing thoughts and faith in some kind of beauty – depict all this with intense, quiet, humble sincerity and make use of whatever you find about you to express yourself, the images from your dreams and the things in your memory. If your everyday life seems to lack material, do not blame it; blame yourself, tell yourself that you are not poet enough to summon up its riches, for there is no lack for him who creates and no poor, trivial place. And even if you were in a prison whose walls did not let any of the sounds of the world outside reach your senses – would you not have your childhood still, this marvellous, lavish source, this treasure-house of memories? Turn your attention towards that. Attempt to raise the sunken sensations of this distant past; your self will become the stronger for it, your loneliness will open up and become a twilit dwelling in which the noise other people make is only heard far off. And if from this turn inwards, from this submersion in your own world, there come *verses*, then it will not occur to you to ask anyone whether they are good verses. Nor will you attempt to interest magazines in these bits of work: for in them you will see your beloved natural possessions, a piece, and a voice, of your life. A work of art is good if it has arisen out of necessity. The verdict on it lies in this nature of its origin: there is no other. For this reason, my dear Sir, the only advice I have is this: to go into yourself and to examine the depths from which your life springs; at its source you will find the answer to the question of whether you *have* to write. Accept this answer as it is, without seeking to interpret it. Perhaps it will turn out that you are called to be an artist. Then assume this fate and bear it, its burden and its greatness, without ever asking after the rewards that may come from outside. For he who creates must be a world of his own and find everything within himself and in the natural world that he has elected to follow.

But perhaps even after this descent into yourself and into your solitariness you will have to give up the idea of becoming a poet (the feeling that one could live without writing is enough, as I said, to make it something one should never do). But even then, to have taken pause in the way I am asking you to will not have been in vain. Whatever happens, your life will find its own paths from that point on, and that they may be good, productive and far-reaching is something I wish for you more than I can say.

What else should I say to you? I think everything has been emphasized as it should be; and all I wanted to do in the end was advise you to go through your development quietly and seriously; you cannot disrupt it more than by looking outwards and expecting answers from without to questions that only your innermost instinct in your quietest moments will perhaps be able to answer.

I was delighted to find Professor Horaček's name in your letter; I retain a great admiration for this kind-hearted scholar, a gratitude that has endured over the years. Could you please pass on these sentiments to him; it is very kind of him still to remember me, and I much appreciate it.

The verses you were so good as to entrust me with I am sending back to you along with this letter. Thank you again for the extent and the warmth of your trust – as well as I can, I have attempted with this sincere reply to make myself a little worthier of it than, as a stranger, I really am.

With all devotion and sympathy,
    Rainer Maria Rilke

You must forgive me, my dear Sir, for only attending to your letter of 24 February today: the whole time I have been under the weather, not ill exactly but oppressed by an influenza-like feebleness which has made me incapable of anything. And in the end, when all else had failed, I travelled down to this southern coast, whose beneficial effects have helped me in the past. But I'm still not well again, writing is difficult, and so you must take these few lines as if there were more of them.

First of all you should know that every letter from you will always be a pleasure, and you only need to be understanding with regard to the replies, which often, maybe, will leave you with empty hands; for at bottom, and particularly in the deepest and most important things, we are unutterably alone, and for one person to be able to advise, let alone help, another, a great deal must come about, a great deal must come right, a whole constellation of things must concur for it to be possible at all.

There are just two things I wanted to say to you today:

Irony: don't let yourself be ruled by it, especially not in uncreative moments. In creative ones try to make use of it as one means among many to get a grasp on life. Used purely, it too is pure, and there is no need to be ashamed of it; and if you feel too familiar with it, if you fear your intimacy is growing too much, then turn towards great and serious subjects, next to which irony becomes small and helpless. Seek out the depths of things: irony will never reach down there – and if in so doing you come up against something truly great, inquire whether this way of relating to things originates in a necessary part of your being. For under the influence of serious things irony will either fall away (if it is something incidental) or on the contrary (if it really belongs to you in a native way) it will gain strength and so become a serious tool and take its place among the means with which you will be bound to create your art.

And the second thing I wanted to tell you today is this:

Of all my books there are only a few I cannot do without, and two are always among my effects, wherever I am. I have them with me here: the Bible, and the books of the great Danish writer *Jens Peter Jacobsen*. I wonder whether you know his works. They are easy to get hold of, because a number of them are available in good translations in Reclam's Universal-Bibliothek. Get hold of the little volume *Six Novellas* by J. P. Jacobsen, and his novel *Niels Lyhne*, and begin with the first story in the first of these volumes which is called 'Mogens'. A world will come over you, the joy, the richness, the incomprehensible greatness of a new world. Live in these books for a while, learn from them what seems to be worth learning, but above all love them. This love will be repaid you thousands and thousands of times, and however your life may turn out – this love, I am sure of it, will run through the weave of your becoming as one of the most important threads of all among the other threads of your experiences, disappointments and joys.

If I had to say from whom I have learnt anything about the nature of artistic creation, about its profundity and eternity, there are only two names I can give: *Jacobsen's*, the great, great poet, and *Auguste Rodin's*, the sculptor who has no equal among all artists now alive. –

All success on your paths!

Yours,

Rainer Maria Rilke

Your Easter letter, my dear Sir, gave me a great deal of pleasure, for it had many good things to report, and the way you spoke about Jacobsen's great and generous art showed me that I was not mistaken in conducting your life and its many questions to this source of plenty.

Now *Niels Lyhne* will reveal itself to you, a book full of splendours and depths; the more often one reads it, it seems to contain everything, from life's faintest scent to the full, grand savour of its heaviest fruits. There is nothing in it that has not been understood, grasped, lived, and known in memory's trembling, lingering resonance; no experience is too slight, and the merest occurrence unfolds like a fate, and fate itself is like a wonderful, vast fabric in which every thread is drawn by an infinitely tender hand and laid next to another, held in place and supported by a hundred others. You will experience the immense pleasure of reading this book for the first time, and will pass through its innumerable surprises as if in a new dream. But I can tell you that later too one always traverses these books with the same astonishment and that they lose nothing of the wondrous power, relinquish none of the magical qualities, which they lavish on the reader the first time round.

One just takes more and more enjoyment in them, one grows ever more grateful and somehow better and simpler in seeing the world, deeper in one's faith in life and happier and larger in living. –

And later you must read the wonderful book of the fate and longings of *Marie Grubbe* and Jacobsen's letters and diaries and fragments and finally his verse which (even if the translations are only moderate) has an infinite resonance. (To do so, I'd suggest you buy the lovely collected edition of Jacobsen's works – which has all this in it – if you get the opportunity. It came out in three volumes and in good translations with Eugen Diederichs in Leipzig and costs, I believe, only 5 or 6 marks a volume.)

In your opinion on 'Here roses should stand ...' (a work of such incomparable subtlety and form) you are of course absolutely in the right, and inviolably so, whatever the author of the preface may have to say. And let me at once make this request: read as little as possible in the way of aesthetics and criticism – it will either be partisan views, fossilized and made meaningless in its lifeless rigidity, or it will be neat wordplay, where one opinion will triumph one day and the opposite the next. Works of art are infinitely solitary and nothing is less likely to reach them than criticism. Only love can grasp them and hold them and do them justice. – With regard to any such disquisition, review or introduction, trust yourself and your instincts; even if you go wrong in your judgement, the natural growth of your inner life will gradually, over time, lead you to other insights. Allow your verdicts their own quiet untroubled development which like all progress must come from deep within and cannot be forced or accelerated. *Everything* must be carried to term before it is born. To let every impression and the germ of every feeling come to completion inside, in the dark, in the unsayable, the unconscious, in what is unattainable to one's own intellect, and to wait with deep humility and patience for the hour when a new clarity is delivered: that alone is to live as an artist, in the understanding and in one's creative work.

These things cannot be measured by time, a year has no meaning, and ten years are nothing. To be an artist means: not to calculate and count; to grow and ripen like a tree which does not hurry the flow of its sap and stands at ease in the spring gales without fearing that no summer may follow. It will come. But it comes only to those who are patient, who are simply there in their vast, quiet tranquillity, as if eternity lay before them. It is a lesson I learn every day amid hardships I am thankful for: *patience* is all!

RICHARD DEHMEL: With his books (as also, by the way, with the man himself whom I know slightly) I always find myself, when I've come upon one of his best pages, fearful of the next, which can always undo it all again and turn what was so lovely into something base. You sum him up very well with your phrase about 'living and writing in rut'. – And indeed artistic experience lies so incredibly close to sexual experience, to its pains and pleasures, that both phenomena are really just different forms of one and the same desire and felicity. And if instead of speaking of 'rut' we could say 'sex', sex in the large, capacious, pure sense, not rendered suspect by any misapprehensions stemming from the Church, his art would be very great and infinitely important. His poetic power is immense, as vigorous as instinct; it has its own reckless rhythms running through it and bursts out of him as if from a mountain.

But this power seems not always to be quite genuine and free of affectation. (But then that is one of the severest tests of an artist: he must always remain innocent and unconscious of his greatest virtues if he is to avoid depriving them of their uninhibitedness and purity.) And when this power, coursing through his being, reaches his sexuality, it doesn't find quite the pure human being it needs. The world of sexuality it finds is not entirely mature and pure, it is not *human* enough, only *virile*, rut, intoxication, restlessness, and weighed down by the old prejudices and arrogance with which men have disfigured and overburdened love. Because he loves *only* as a man, not as a human being, there is in his sense of sexuality something narrow, seemingly savage, hateful, time-bound, uneternal that diminishes his art and makes it ambivalent and doubtful. It is not without blemish, it is marked by the times and by passion, and little of it will prevail and endure. (But that's the case with most art!) In spite of all this one can still take deep pleasure in what is great about his work and must just make sure not to lose oneself to it and become an acolyte of this Dehmel-world which is so full of anxiety, of adultery and confusion, and remote from the real destinies, which create more suffering than these passing afflictions but also give more opportunity for greatness and more courage to make something that will last.

To come to my own books, really I'd like to send you all those that might give pleasure. But I am very poor, and as soon as my books have appeared they cease to belong to me. I cannot buy them myself and, as I'd so often like to, give them to those who would value and look after them.

For that reason I have written down for you on a slip of paper the titles (and publishing houses) of my recent books (that is the very newest, altogether I must have

published 12 or 13) and must leave it to you, dear Sir, to
order one or two of them if they take your fancy.

I shall be glad to know that my books are with you.

All good wishes,

   Yours,

     Rainer Maria Rilke

About ten days ago I left Paris, ailing and very weary, and travelled to these great northern plains whose vastness and quiet and sky are supposed to return my health to me. But I drove into unceasing rain which only today is beginning to clear a bit over the restless, windswept land; and I'm using this first moment of brightness to send you a greeting, my dear Sir.

My dear Mr Kappus: I have left your letter unanswered for a long time – not that I had forgotten it; on the contrary, it was the kind of letter one reads again, coming across it among one's papers, and I recognized you in it as if I were in your presence. It was your letter of the second of May – I'm sure you remember it. When, as I do now, I read it in the great calm of these expanses, I am touched by your fine concern for life, even more than I was in Paris where everything has a different tone and gets lost in the immense din which sets things trembling. Here, surrounded as I am by a mighty stretch of land over which the winds blow in from seas, here I feel that no human being anywhere can respond to those questions and feelings that have a profound life of their own; for even the best of us get the words wrong when we want them to express such intangible and almost unsayable things. But all the same I believe that you need not remain without solution if you hold to things like those now refreshing my eyes. If you hold close to nature, to what is simple in it, to the small things people hardly see and which all of a sudden can become great and immeasurable; if you have this love for what is slight, and quite unassumingly, as a

servant, seek to win the confidence of what seems poor –
then everything will grow easier, more unified and
somehow more conciliatory, not perhaps in the intellect,
which, amazed, remains a step behind, but in your deep-
est consciousness, watchfulness and knowledge. You are
so young, all still lies ahead of you, and I should like to
ask you, as best I can, dear Sir, to be patient towards all
that is unresolved in your heart and to try to love *the
questions themselves* like locked rooms, like books writ-
ten in a foreign tongue. Do not now strive to uncover
answers: they cannot be given you because you have not
been able to live them. And what matters is to live every-
thing. *Live* the questions for now. Perhaps then you will
gradually, without noticing it, live your way into the
answer, one distant day in the future. Perhaps you do
carry within yourself the possibility of forming and creat-
ing, as a particularly happy and pure way of living. School
yourself for it, but take what comes in complete trust, and
as long as it is a product of your will, of some kind of
inner necessity, accept it and do not despise it. Sex is dif-
ficult, true. But difficult things are what we were set to do,
almost everything serious is difficult, and everything is
serious. If you only acknowledge this and manage from
your own resources, from your own disposition and
nature, from your own experience and childhood and
strength, to win your way towards a relationship to sex
that is wholly your own (*not* influenced by convention
and custom), then you have no need to fear losing your-
self and becoming unworthy of your best possession.

Physical desire is a sensual experience, no different
from pure contemplation or the pure sensation with
which a fine fruit sates the tongue; it is a great and endless

feeling which is granted to us, a way of knowing the world, the fullness and the splendour of all knowledge. And that we receive this pleasure cannot be a bad thing; what is bad is the way almost all of us misuse the experience and waste it and apply it as a stimulus to the tired parts of our lives, as a distraction instead of as a concentration of ourselves into climactic points. Eating, too, has been turned away from its true nature: want on the one hand and superfluity on the other have troubled the clarity of this need, and all the profound, simple necessities in which life renews itself have similarly been obscured. But the individual can clarify them for himself and live in this clearness (and if not the individual, who is too dependent, then at least the solitary). He can remind himself that all beauty in plants and animals is a quiet and durable form of love and longing, and he can see the animal, as also the plant, patiently and willingly joining and multiplying and growing, not from physical pleasure, not from physical suffering, but bowing to necessities which are greater than pleasure and pain and more powerful than desire and resistance. Oh if only mankind could embrace this mystery, which penetrates the earth right into its smallest elements, with more humility, and bear and sustain it with more gravity and know how terribly heavy it is, instead of taking it lightly. If only mankind could hold its own fertility in awe, which is one and the same whether it manifests itself in the spirit or in the flesh. For creativity of the spirit has its origin in the physical kind, is of one nature with it and only a more delicate, more rapt and less fleeting version of the carnal sort of sex. 'The desire to be a creator, to engender, to give form' is nothing without its continuing, palpable confirmation and realization in the world,

nothing without the myriad expressions of assent coming
from animals and things. And the pleasure it gives is only
as unutterably fine and abundant as it is because it is full
of inherited memories of the engendering and bearing of
millions. In one creative thought a thousand forgotten
nights of love revive and lend it grandeur and height. And
those who come together in the night-time and are
entwined in a cradle of desire are carrying out a serious
work in collecting sweetness, profundity and strength for
the song of some poet yet to come, who will rise up to
speak unutterable pleasures. And they summon up the
future; and even if they err and embrace one another
blindly, the future will come all the same, a new creature
will appear, and based on the chance act that seems to be
accomplished here the law comes into being according to
which a resistant and vigorous seed forces its way through
to the egg moving forward to receive it. Do not be dis-
tracted by surfaces; it is in the depths that all laws obtain.
And those who live the mystery falsely and badly (and
there are many of them) forfeit it only for themselves and
still hand it on like a sealed letter, unwittingly. And don't
be put off by the multiplicity of names and the complex-
ity of the various cases. Perhaps a great maternity lies
over everything, as a shared longing. The beauty of the
virgin, of a being, who, as you put it so well, 'has not yet
achieved anything', is maternity divining and preparing
itself, anxious and full of longing. And the beauty of a
mother is maternity at work, and that of the old woman
a great memory. And in the man too there is maternity, as
it seems to me, physical and spiritual; his engendering is
also a kind of giving birth, and it is an act of birth when
he creates out of his inmost resources. And perhaps the

sexes are more closely related than we think, and the great renewal of the world will perhaps consist in man and woman, freed of all sense of error and disappointment, seeking one another out not as opposites but as brothers and sisters and neighbours, and they will join together as *human beings*, to share the heavy weight of sexuality that is laid upon them with simplicity, gravity and patience.

But everything which one day will perhaps be possible for many, the solitary individual can prepare for and build now with his hands which are more unerring. For this reason, dear Mr Kappus, love your solitude and bear the pain it causes you with melody wrought with lament. For the people who are close to you, you tell me, are far away, and that shows that you are beginning to create a wider space around you. And if what is close is far, then the space around you is wide indeed and already among the stars; take pleasure in your growth, in which no one can accompany you, and be kind-hearted towards those you leave behind, and be assured and gentle with them and do not plague them with your doubts or frighten them with your confidence or your joyfulness, which they cannot understand. Look for some kind of simple and loyal way of being together with them which does not necessarily have to alter however much you may change; love in them a form of life different from your own and show under-standing for the older ones who fear precisely the solitude in which you trust. Avoid providing material for the drama which always spans between parents and their children; it saps much of the children's strength and con-sumes that parental love which works and warms even when it does not comprehend. Ask no advice of them and reckon with no understanding; but believe in a love which is stored up for you like an inheritance, and trust that in this love there is a strength and a benediction out of whose sphere you do not need to issue even if your journey is a long one.

It is good that for the moment you are going into a profession which will make you independent and mean you only have yourself to rely on, in every sense. Have the patience to wait and see whether your inmost life feels confined by the form of this occupation. I consider it a very difficult and a very demanding one, as it is burdened by powerful conventions and leaves almost no room to interpret its duties according to your own lights. But your solitude, even in the midst of quite foreign circumstances, will be a hold and a home for you, and leading from it you will find all the paths you need. All my good wishes are ready to accompany you, and you have all my confidence and trust.

Yours,
Rainer Maria Rilke

My dear Sir,

Your letter of 29 August reached me in Florence, and only now – two months on – do I give you news of it. Forgive me this delay, but I prefer not to write letters when I'm travelling because letter-writing requires more of me than just the basic wherewithal: some quiet and time on my own and a moment when I feel relatively at home.

We arrived in Rome about six weeks ago, at a time when it was still the empty, hot city, the Rome supposedly ridden with fevers, and this circumstance, together with other practical difficulties to do with settling in, meant that the unrest surrounding us went on and on and the foreignness of the place lay on us with the weight of homelessness. On top of that you have to remember that Rome (if one is not yet acquainted with it) seems oppressively sad when one first arrives: the lifeless and drear museum-atmosphere it breathes, the abundance of fragments of the past (on which a tiny present nourishes itself) that have been fetched out of the ground and laboriously maintained, the unspeakable excess of esteem, nourished by academics and philologists with the help of run-of-the-mill tourists, given to all these disfigured and spoilt objects which after all are basically nothing more than accidental vestiges of another age and of a life that is not our own and is not meant to be. At last, after weeks of daily fending off, you get your bearings back, and somewhat dazed you tell yourself: No, there is not *more* beauty here than elsewhere, and all these objects which generation after generation have continued to admire, which inexpert hands have mended and restored, they mean nothing, are nothing and have no heart and no value; but there is a great deal of beauty here, because there is beauty everywhere. Infinitely lively waters go over the old aqueducts into the city and on the many squares dance over bowls of white stone and fill broad capacious basins and murmur all day and raise their murmur into the night, which is vast and starry and soft with winds. And there are gardens here, unforgettable avenues and flights of steps, steps conceived by Michelangelo, steps built to resemble cascades of flowing water – giving birth to step after broad step like wave after wave as they descend the incline. With the help of such impressions you regain your composure, win your way back out of the demands of the talking and chattering multitude (how voluble it is!), and you slowly learn to recognize the very few things in which something everlasting can be felt, something you can love, something solitary in which you can take part in silence.

I'm still living in the city, on the Capitol, not far from the finest equestrian statue that has come down to us from Roman art – that of Marcus Aurelius. But in a few weeks I shall be moving into a quiet, simple room, an old summer-house lost in the depths of a great park, hidden away from the city with its noise and its inconsequentiality. I'll live there for the whole winter and take pleasure in the great stillness from which I expect the gift of good and productive hours ...

From there, where I shall feel more at home, I'll write you a longer letter in which I'll also have something to say about your writing. Today I must just mention (and it was perhaps wrong of me not to have done so before) that the book you announced in your letter (which you said contained pieces by you) has not arrived here. Has it been sent back to you, perhaps from Worpswede? (For: packets cannot be forwarded abroad.) This is the best explanation, which it would be nice to have confirmed. I hope it has not gone astray, which given the Italian postal service cannot be ruled out – alas.

I should have been glad to receive the book (as with everything that gives some sign of you); and any verse you have written since I shall always (if you entrust me with it) read and reread and take in as well and as completely as I can. With good wishes and greetings,

Yours,

Rainer Maria Rilke

My dear Mr Kappus,

You shall not go without greetings from me at Christmas time, when you are perhaps finding your solitude harder than usual to bear among all the festivities. But if you notice that it is great, then be glad of it; for what (you must ask yourself) would a solitude be that was not great? There is only *one* solitude, and it is vast and not easy to bear and almost everyone has moments when they would happily exchange it for some form of company, be it ever so banal or trivial, for the illusion of some slight correspondence with whoever one happens to come across, however unworthy ... But perhaps those are precisely the hours when solitude grows, for its growth is painful like the growth of boys and sad like the beginning of spring. But that must not put you off. What is needed is this, and this alone: solitude, great inner loneliness. Going into oneself and not meeting anyone for hours – that is what one must arrive at. Loneliness of the kind one knew as a child, when the grown-ups went back and forth bound up in things which seemed grave and weighty because they looked so busy, and because one had no idea what they were up to.

And when one day you realize that their preoccupations are meagre, their professions barren and no longer connected to life, why not continue to look on them like a child, as if on something alien, drawing on the depths of your own world, on the expanse of your own solitude, which itself is work and achievement and a vocation?

Why wish to exchange a child's wise incomprehension for rejection and contempt, when incomprehension is solitude, whereas rejection and contempt are ways of participating in what, by precisely these means, you want to sever yourself from?

Think, dear Mr Kappus, of the world that you carry within you, and call this thinking whatever you like. Whether it is memory of your own childhood or longing for your own future – just be attentive towards what rises up inside you, and place it above everything that you notice round about. What goes on in your innermost being is worth all your love, this is what you must work on however you can and not waste too much time and too much energy on clarifying your attitude to other people. Who says you have such an attitude at all? – I know, your profession is hard and goes against you, and I had foreseen your complaints and knew they would come. Now that they have come I cannot assuage them; I can only advise you to consider whether all professions are not like that, full of demands, full of hostility for the individual, steeped as it were in the hatred of those who with sullen resentment have settled for a life of sober duty. The station you are now obliged to occupy is no more heavily burdened with conventions, prejudices and misapprehensions than any other, and if there are some domains that make a show of greater freedom there are none that are vast and spacious and in contact with the great things of which real life consists. Only the solitary individual is subject, like a thing, to the fundamental laws, and if someone goes out into the morning as it is breaking, or looks out into the evening full of occurrence, and if he feels what is happening there, every hint of station slips from him as if from a dead man, although he is standing in the midst of life itself. Dear Mr Kappus, something similar to what you now have to undergo as an officer would have affected you in any of the existing professions, and even if, outside of any position, you had sought only fleeting and non-committal contact with society, you would not have been spared this feeling of constraint. – It is the same everywhere; but that is no reason for anxiety or sadness; if there is no communal feeling between you and other people, try to be near to things – they will not abandon you. The nights are still there and the winds that go through the trees and over the many lands; among things and among animals all is still full of happenings in which you can take part; and the children are still as you were when you were a child, just as sad and happy, and whenever you think of your childhood you live among them again, among the lonely children, and adults are nothing and their dignity has no worth.

And if it frightens and pains you to think of your childhood and of the simplicity and stillness that go together with it, because you can no longer believe in God, who is everywhere present in it, then ask yourself, dear Mr Kappus, whether you have really lost God after all? Is it not rather the case that you have never yet possessed him? For when was it supposed to have been? Do you think a child can hold him, him whom grown men only bear with difficulty and whose weight bows down the old? Do you believe that anyone who really has him could lose him like a little pebble, or don't you think that whoever had him could only be lost by him alone? – But if you acknowledge that he was not present in your childhood, and not before that, if you suspect that Christ was deceived by his longing and Mohammed betrayed by his pride, and if you feel with horror that even now he is not present, at the moment when we are talking about him, what then gives you the right to miss him who never was, as if he had disappeared, and to search for him as if he were lost?

Why don't you think of him as a coming god, who since eternity has lain ahead of us, the future one, the eventual fruit of a tree of which we are the leaves? What prevents you from casting his birth out into the times of becoming and from living your life like a painful and beautiful day in the history of a great pregnancy? Don't you see how everything that happens is always a beginning again, and could it not be *His* beginning, given that beginnings are in themselves always so beautiful? If he is the complete being, must not slighter things come before him, so that he can pick himself out of fullness and abundance? – Must he not be the last in order to encompass all things in himself, and what significance would we have if the one whom we hanker for had already been?

As the bees collect honey together, so we fetch the sweetness out of everything and build *Him*. We begin with the very slightest things, with what is barely noticeable (as long as it comes about through love), with our work and the repose that comes after, with a moment of silence or with a small solitary joy, with everything that we do on our own without helpers and accomplices, we begin him whom we shall never know, just as our ancestors could not live to know us. And yet they are in us, these people long since passed away, as a disposition, as a load weighing on our destinies, as a murmur in the blood and as a gesture that rises up out of the depths of time.

Is there anything that can strip you of the hope of dwelling one day in him, the most remote, the most extreme?

Dear Mr Kappus, celebrate Christmas in the piety of the feeling that He perhaps requires of you precisely this existential anxiety in order to begin. Precisely these days of transition are perhaps the period when everything in you is working on him, just as before, as a child, you worked on him with bated breath. Be patient and even-tempered and remember that the least we can do is not make his becoming more difficult than the earth makes it for spring when it decides to come.

And I wish you happiness and confidence.

Yours,

Rainer Maria Rilke

My dear Mr Kappus,

Much time has gone past since I received your last letter. Don't hold that against me; first it was work, then disruptions and finally ill-health that kept me from replying, whereas I wanted to write to you out of good, peaceful days. Now I feel a little better again (even here the beginning of spring with its bad and fickle transitions was hard to bear) and can manage to send you greetings, dear Mr Kappus, and (as I am very glad to do) say this and that about your letter, as best I can.

You will see: I have copied out your sonnet because I found that it had beauty and simplicity and a native form in which it unfolds with such quiet propriety. It is the best of the verses of yours I have been permitted to read. And I'm giving you this copy now because I know that it is important and a whole new experience to come across a work of one's own in a foreign hand. Read the lines as if they were unknown to you, and you will feel in your inmost self how very much they are yours. –

It has been a pleasure for me to read this sonnet and your letter, which I did often. I thank you for both.

And you must not let yourself be diverted out of your solitude by the fact that something in you wants to escape from it. Precisely this desire, if you use it calmly and judiciously, as a kind of tool, will help you to extend your solitude over a greater expanse of ground. People have tended (with the help of conventions) to resolve everything in the direction of easiness, of the light, and on the lightest side of the light; but it is clear that we must hold to the heavy, the difficult. All living things do this, everything in nature grows and defends itself according to its kind and is a distinct creature from out of its own resources, strives to be so at any cost and in the face of all resistance. We know little, but that we must hold fast to what is difficult is a certainty that will never forsake us. It is good to be alone, for solitude is difficult; that something is difficult should be one more reason to do it.

To love is also good, for love is hard. Love between one person and another: that is perhaps the hardest thing it is laid on us to do, the utmost, the ultimate trial and test, the work for which all other work is just preparation. For this reason young people, who are beginners in everything, do not yet *know* how to love: they must learn. With their whole being, with all their strength, concerted on their solitary, fearful, upward beating hearts, they have to learn to love. An apprenticeship though is always a long, secluded period, and love too is for a great long time and far into life: solitariness, heightened and deepened loneliness for the one in love. Love at first has nothing to do with unfolding, abandon and uniting with another person (for what would be the sense in a union of what is unrefined and unfinished, still second order?); for the individual it is a grand opportunity to mature, to become something in himself, to become a world, to become a world in himself for another's sake; it is a great immoderate demand made upon the self, something that singles him out and summons him to vast designs. Only in this sense, as a duty to work on themselves ('to hearken and to hammer day and night'), should young people use the love that is given them. The unfolding, the abandon and any kind of togetherness is not for them (who for a long time yet will have to scrimp and save). They are the culmination, and perhaps that for which a human life now is hardly sufficient.

But there young people so often and so badly go wrong: in that they (who by nature have no patience) fling themselves at one another when love comes over them, scatter themselves just as they are in all their troubledness, disorder, confusion ... But what can come of that? What is life supposed to do with this heap of half-broken things that they call their togetherness and would like to call their happiness, were it possible, their future? Each person loses himself then for the other's sake and loses the other and many more who were yet to come. And loses the expanses and possibilities, exchanges the nearing and fleeing of delicate, mysterious things for a sterile helplessness of which nothing more can come; nothing but a bit of disgust, disappointment and deprivation and the escape into one of the many conventions which like public shelters are set up in great numbers along this most dangerous of paths. No area of human experience is so well furnished with conventions as this: there are lifebelts of the most various invention, dinghies and buoyancy devices; society in its wisdom has found ways of constructing refuges of all kinds, for since it has been disposed to make the love-life a pastime, it has also felt obliged to trivialize it, to make it cheap, risk-free and secure, as public pleasures usually are.

It is true that many young people who love wrongly, that is, simply with abandon and not in solitude (and your average person will never move beyond this), feel the oppression of having failed at something and do want to make the state into which they have got liveable and productive in their own, personal way; for their nature tells them that questions of love, even less than all other important matters, cannot be solved publicly and by following this or that consensus; that they are questions that touch the quick of what it is to be human and which in every case require a new, particular and *purely* private response: but how can people who have already flung together and no longer set themselves any limits or tell one another apart, and who therefore possess nothing of their own any more, how on earth can they find a way out of themselves, out of the depths of a solitude that has already been spilt and squandered?

They act out of a shared helplessness, and if they do their best to escape the convention they happen to have noticed (as marriage for example), they fall into the clutches of a less obvious but just as deadly conventional solution; for all around them there is nothing but – convention; when an action derives from a precipitately arrived at and unwitting union, it is *always* conventional; every relationship which is the product of such confusion has its conventions, however unusual (that is, immoral in the generally accepted sense) it may be; yes, even separation would in such a case be a conventional step, an impersonal, fortuitous decision without force and without point.

Whoever looks at the matter seriously finds that, as for death, which is difficult, no explanation, no solution, has yet been discovered for love, which is difficult too: there are no directions, no path. And for these two problems that we carry round with us in a sealed packet and hand on without opening, it will always be impossible to locate a common rule, resting on consensus. But to the same extent that we begin as individuals to venture onto life, these great things will encounter us, on our own, at ever closer quarters. The demands that the hard work of love makes on our development are larger than life, and as beginners we are not a match for them. But if we can hold out and take this love upon us as a burden and an apprenticeship, instead of losing ourselves in all the trivial and frivolous games behind which people have hidden from the utter seriousness of their existence, then perhaps a small advance and some relief will be sensible to those who come long after us. That would mean a great deal.

We are only now just coming to the point where we can consider the relationship of one human individual to another objectively and without prejudice, and our attempts to live such a relation have no model to go on. And yet in the shifting of the times there are already a few things that can help our tentative beginnings.

Girls and women, in their new, particular unfolding, will only in passing imitate men's behaviour and misbehaviour and follow in male professions. Once the uncertainty of such transitions is over it will emerge that women have only passed through the spectrum and the variety of those (often laughable) disguises in order to purify their truest natures from the distorting influences of the other sex. Women, in whom life abides and dwells more immediately, more fruitfully and more trustingly, are bound to have ripened more thoroughly, become more human human beings, than a man, who is all too light and has not been pulled down beneath the surface of life by the weight of a bodily fruit and who, in his arrogance and impatience, undervalues what he thinks he loves. This humanity which inhabits woman, brought to term in pain and humiliation, will, once she has shrugged off the conventions of mere femininity through the transformations of her outward status, come clearly to light, and men, who today do not yet feel it approaching, will be taken by surprise and struck down by it. One day (there are already reliable signs which speak for it and which begin to spread their light, especially in the northern countries), one day there will be girls and women whose name will no longer just signify the opposite of the male but something in their own right, something which does not make one think of any supplement or limit but only of life and existence: the female human being.

This step forward (at first right against the will of the men who are left behind) will transform the experience of love, which is now full of error, alter it root and branch, reshape it into a relation between two human beings and no longer between man and woman. And this more human form of love (which will be performed in infinitely gentle and considerate fashion, true and clear in its creating of bonds and dissolving of them) will resemble the one we are struggling and toiling to prepare the way for, the love that consists in two solitudes protecting, defining and welcoming one another.

And one more thing: do not believe that that abundance of love which was once, as a boy, bestowed on you is now lost. Can you tell whether back then great and good desires did not ripen within you, and resolutions which you still live by today? I believe that love remains so strong and powerful in your memory because it was your first deep experience of solitariness and the first

inner work that you undertook on your life. – All good
wishes to you, dear Mr Kappus!

  Yours,

   Rainer Maria Rilke

Sonnet

Through my life there trembles unlamenting
suffering dark and deep, without a sigh.
Pure as snow the blossoming of my dreams
consecrates the stillest of my days.

Often though a question's gravity
cuts across my path. I seem to shrink,
pass coldly on as if beside a lake
whose waters are too vast for me to measure.

And then a sadness settles, dim, opaque,
like the grey of pallid summer nights,
shimmered through with stars – now and then – :

love then is what my hands attempt to grasp
because I want to say a prayer whose sounds
my burning mouth, my lips, cannot bring forth ...

                         (Franz Kappus)

Borgeby gård, Flãdie, Sweden, 12 August 1904

I want to talk to you again for a while, dear Mr Kappus, although I can say almost nothing that is of any help, hardly anything useful. You have had many great sadnesses which have now passed by. And you say that their passing was also hard and upsetting for you. But I ask you to consider whether these great unhappinesses did not rather pass *through* you. Whether much within you has not changed, whether somewhere, in some part of your being, you were not transformed while you were unhappy? The only sorrows which are harmful and bad are those one takes among people in order to drown them out. Like diseases which are treated superficially and inexpertly, they only abate, and after a short pause break out again with more terrible force, and accumulate inside and are life, unlived, rejected, lost life – from which we can die. If it were possible for us to see further than our knowledge reaches, and a little beyond the outworks of our intuitions, perhaps we should then bear our sadnesses with greater assurance than our joys. For they are the moments when something new enters into us, something unknown to us; our feelings, shy and inhibited, fall silent, everything in us withdraws, a stillness settles on us, and at the centre of it is the new presence that nobody yet knows, making no sound.

I believe that almost all our sadnesses are periods of tautening that we experience as numbness because we can no longer hear the stirring of our feelings, which have become foreign to us. Because we are alone with the strange thing that has entered into us; because everything familiar and accustomed is taken away from us for a moment; because we are in the middle of a transition where we cannot stand still. And that is why sadness passes: what is new in us, the thing that has supervened, has entered into our heart, penetrated to its innermost chamber and not lingered even there – it is already in our blood. And we never quite know what it was. One might easily suppose that nothing had happened, but we have altered the way a house alters when a guest enters it. We cannot say who has come, perhaps we shall never know, but there are many indications that it is the future that enters into us like this, in order to be transformed within us, long before it actually occurs. And that is why it is so important to be solitary and attentive when one is sad: because the apparently uneventful and static moment when our future comes upon us is so much closer to life than that other noisy and accidental point when it happens to us as if from the outside. The quieter, the more patient and open we are in our sadness, the deeper and more unerringly the new will penetrate into us, the better we shall acquire it, the more it will be *our* fate, and when one day in the future it 'takes place' (that is, steps out of us towards others) we shall feel related and close to it in our inmost hearts. And that is necessary. It is necessary – and little by little our development will tend in this direction – that nothing alien should happen to us, but only what has long been part of us. We have already had to adjust our understanding of so many theories of planetary motion, and so too we shall gradually learn to recognize that what we call fate originates in ourselves, in humankind, and does not work on us from the outside. Only because so many people did not absorb their fates while they were inhabited by them, and did not make them a part of themselves, only because of this did they fail to recognize what emerged from them. It was so foreign to them that in their confused panic they assumed it must just have entered into them, for they swore never to have found anything of the sort in themselves before. Just as for a long time people were deceived about the movement of the sun, so we are still deceived about the movement of what is to come. The future is fixed, dear Mr Kappus, but we move around in infinite space.

How could things not be difficult for us?

And if we come back to solitude, it grows ever clearer that fundamentally it is not something that one can take or leave. We *are* solitary. It is possible to deceive yourself and act as if it were not the case. That is all. How much better though, to see and accept that that is what we are, and even to take it as our starting-point. If we do, the effect is admittedly one of giddiness; for all the points on which we are accustomed to rest our eyes are taken away from us, there is no longer anything close by, and everything remote is infinitely so. Someone transported from his room, almost without warning and interval, onto the top of a high mountain would feel something like it: he would be virtually destroyed by an unparalleled sense of insecurity, by an exposure to something nameless. He would think he was falling or believe himself to be hurtling out into space or shattered into a thousand pieces: what a monstrous lie his brain would have to invent to rein in and clarify the state of his senses. In the same way all distances, all measurements, alter for the one who becomes solitary; many such changes suddenly take place at once and, as with the man on the mountain-top, unusual imaginings and curious sensations occur which seem to take on dimensions greater than can be tolerated. But it is necessary for us to experience this too. We must accept our existence in as *wide* a sense as can be; everything, even the unheard-of, must be possible within it. That, when you come down to it, is the only kind of courage that is demanded of us: the courage for the oddest, the most unexpected, the most inexplicable things that we may encounter. That human beings have been cowardly in this regard has done life endless harm; the experiences we describe as 'apparitions', the entire so-called 'spirit world', death, all those things so closely akin to us have by our daily rejection of them been forced so far out of our lives that the senses with which we might apprehend them have atrophied. To say nothing of God. But the fear of the inexplicable has not just rendered the individual existence poorer; relations *between* people, too, have been restricted, as it were lifted out of the river-bed of endless possibilities and placed on a deserted bank where nothing happens. For it is not lethargy alone which causes human relationships to repeat themselves in the same old way with such unspeakable monotony in instance after instance; it is the fearful shying away from any kind of new, unforeseeable experience which we think we may not be equal to. But only someone who is ready for anything and rules nothing out, not even the most enigmatic things, will experience the relationship with another as a living thing and will himself live his own existence to the full. For imagining an individual's existence as a larger or smaller room reveals to us that most people are only acquainted with one corner of their particular room, a place by the window, a little area to pace up and down.

That way, they have a certain security. And yet the peril-ous uncertainty that drives the prisoners in Poe's tales to grope out the outlines of their terrible dungeons and so to know the unspeakable horrors of their surroundings, is so much more human. But we are not prisoners. There are no traps or snares set up around us, and there is nothing that should frighten or torment us. We are placed into life as into the element with which we have the most affinity, and moreover we have after thousands of years of adap-tation come to resemble this life so closely that if we keep still we can, thanks to our facility for mimicry, hardly be distinguished from all that surrounds us. We have no reason to be mistrustful of our world, for it is not against us. If it holds terrors they are *our* terrors, if it has its abysses these abysses belong to us, if there are dangers then we must try to love them. And if we only organize our life according to the principle which teaches us always to hold to what is difficult, then what now still appears most foreign will become our most intimate and most reliable experience. How can we forget those ancient myths found at the beginnings of all peoples? The myths about the dragons who at the last moment turn into prin-cesses? Perhaps all the dragons in our lives are princesses, only waiting for the day when they will see us handsome and brave? Perhaps everything terrifying is deep down a helpless thing that needs our help.

So, dear Mr Kappus, you shouldn't be dismayed if a sadness rises up in front of you, greater than any you have ever seen before; or if a disquiet plays over your hands and over all your doings like light and cloud-shadow. You must think that something is happening with you, that life has not forgotten you, that it holds you in its hand; it will not let you fall. Why should you want to exclude from your life all unsettling, all pain, all depression of spirit, when you don't know what work it is these states are performing within you? Why do you want to persecute yourself with the question of where it all comes from and where it is leading? You well know you are in a period of transition and want nothing more than to be transformed. If there is something ailing in the way you go about things, then remember that sickness is the means by which an organism rids itself of something foreign to it. All one has to do is help it to be ill, to have its whole illness and let it break out, for that is how it mends itself. There is so much, my dear Mr Kappus, going on in you now. You must be patient as an invalid and trusting as a convalescent, for you are perhaps both. And more than that: you are also the doctor responsible for looking after himself. But with all illnesses there are many days when the doctor can do nothing but wait. And inasfar as you are your own doctor, this above all is what you must do now.

Do not watch yourself too closely. Do not draw over-rapid conclusions from what is happening to you. Simply let it happen. Otherwise you will too readily find yourself looking on your past, which is of course not uninvolved with everything that is going on in you now, reproach-fully (that is, moralistically). But what now affects you from among the divagations, desires and longings of your boyhood is not what you will recall and condemn. The extraordinary circumstances of a solitary and helpless childhood are so difficult, so complicated, exposed to so many influences and at the same time removed from any real life-context, that if a vice enters into it we must not be too quick to call it a vice. We should in general be very careful with names; it is so often the name of a crime which destroys a life, not the nameless and personal act itself, which was perhaps completely necessary to that life and could have been absorbed by it without difficulty. And the expenditure of energy only seems so great because you put too much importance on the victory. It is not victory that is the 'great thing' you think you have achieved, though the feeling itself is not in error. What is great is that there was already something there that you were able to set in place of that deception, something true and real. Without it, your victory would only have been a moral reaction with no further significance, but as it is it has become a segment of your life. Of your life, dear Mr Kappus, which I am thinking of with so many hopes and wishes. Do you remember how this life of yours longed in childhood to belong to the 'grown-ups'? I can see that it now longs to move on from them and is drawn to those who are greater yet. That is why it does not cease to be difficult, but also why it will not cease to grow.

And if I have anything else to say to you it is this: do not think that the person who is trying to console you lives effortlessly among the simple, quiet words that sometimes make you feel better. His life is full of troubles and sadness and falls far short of them. But if it were any different he could never have found the words that he did.

Yours,
    Rainer Maria Rilke

My dear Mr Kappus,

During this time that has passed without a letter I was partly travelling and partly too busy to be able to write. And even today writing is not going to be easy because I have had to write a good number of letters already and my hand is tired. If I had someone to dictate to I'd have plenty to say, but as it is you'll have to make do with just a few words in return for your long letter.

I think of you often, dear Mr Kappus, and with such a concentration of good wishes that really in some way it ought to help. Whether my letters can really be a help to you, well, I have my doubts. Do not say: Yes, they are. Just let them sink in quietly and without any particular sense of gratitude, and let's wait and see what will come of it.

There's not perhaps much purpose in my dealing with the detail of what you wrote, for what I might be able to say about your tendency towards self-doubt or your inability to reconcile your inner and outer life, or about anything else that assails you – it all comes down to what I have said before: the same desire that you might find enough patience in you to endure, and simplicity enough to have faith; that you might gain more and more trust in what is hard and in your own loneliness among other people. And otherwise let life take its course. Believe me: life is right, whatever happens.

And as to feelings: all feelings are pure that focus you and raise you up. An impure feeling is one that only comprises *one* side of your nature and so distorts you. Any thoughts that match up to your childhood are good. Everything that makes *more* of you than you have hitherto been in your best moments is right. Every heightening is good if it occurs in the quick of your bloodstream, if it is not an intoxication, not a troubling but a joy one can see right to the bottom of. Do you understand what I mean?

And your doubts can become a good quality if you *school* them. They must grow to be *knowledgeable*, they must learn to be critical. As soon as they begin to spoil something for you ask them *why* a thing is ugly, demand hard evidence, test them, and you will perhaps find them at a loss and short of an answer, or perhaps mutinous. But do not give in, request arguments, and act with this kind of attentiveness and consistency every single time, and the day will come when instead of being demolishers they will be among your best workers – perhaps the canniest of all those at work on the building of your life.

That is all, dear Mr Kappus, that I can say to you for today. But I'm also sending you the off-print of a little work that has just appeared in the Prague journal *Deutsche Arbeit*. There I continue to speak to you of life and of death and of the greatness and splendour of both.

Yours,
    Rainer Maria Rilke

Paris, on the second day of Christmas 1908

You ought to know, dear Mr Kappus, how happy I was to get this lovely letter from you. The news you give me, actual and articulate as it now is, seems good to me, and the more I thought about it the more it struck me as incontrovertibly good. I really wanted to write you this in time for Christmas Eve; but what with the work that has been occupying me variously and without interruption this winter the old festival came up so quickly that I hardly had time enough to make the most necessary purchases, much less to write a letter.

But during these Christmas days I have often thought of you and imagined how quiet you must be in your solitary fort up among the empty mountains over which those great south winds rush as if they wanted to devour them in mighty chunks.

The silence must be immense to be able to receive such sounds and movements, and when one thinks that they are joined by the noise of the sea, present in the distance, perhaps the most inward note in this prehistoric harmony, one can only hope that you have the trust and patience to let this marvellous solitude work on you, a solitude which will never be deleted from your life. In all that lies before you to experience and do, it will continue as an anonymous influence and have a subtly decisive effect, perhaps like the way the blood of our ancestors moves unceasingly within us and mingles with our own to make us the unique, not-to-be-repeated being that we are at every turn of our lives.

Yes: I am glad that you have this firm, utterable form of existence, the rank, the uniform, the duty, all these tangible and well-defined things that in such surroundings, with an equally isolated and not numerous company of men, take on a seriousness and necessity; and which, over and above the aspects of play and pastime that are also part of the military profession, make for a certain vigilance and not only permit an individual attentiveness but actually teach it. And to be in circumstances that work on us, that set us before great natural phenomena from time to time, is all we need.

Art too is only a way of living, and it is possible, however one lives, to prepare oneself for it without knowing; in every real situation we are nearer to it, better neighbours, than in the unreal half-artistic professions which by pretending to be close to art in fact deny and hurt its very existence, as for example is the case with the whole of journalism and almost all criticism and three-quarters of what passes for literature. I am glad, in a word, that you have withstood the dangers of slipping into all this, and that somewhere you are living alone and courageous in a rough reality. May the year to come maintain and strengthen you in it.

Ever yours,
R. M. Rilke

THE LETTER FROM THE
YOUNG WORKER

At a gathering last Thursday there was a reading of your poems, Mr V., it haunts me still; the only thing I can think to do is set down for you what is preoccupying me, inasmuch as it is possible for me to do so.

The day after the reading I found myself by chance at a Christian meeting, and perhaps it was this that really set things off and caused the detonation that has released so much commotion and energy that I am now heading towards you with all my faculties. It is a monstrous act of violence to begin something. I cannot *begin*. I'm simply jumping over what ought to be the beginning. Nothing is as powerful as silence. Were we not all of us born into talk, it would never have been broken.

Mr V., I am not speaking of the evening when we heard your poems. I am speaking of the other one. I am driven to say: who – yes, I can find no other way of expressing it now – *who* then is this Christ who meddles with everything. Who knows nothing about us, nothing about our work, nothing about our needs, nothing about our joys as we achieve, go through and summon them up nowadays – and who nevertheless, it seems, always demands to be the *first* person in our life. Or are these things just words put in his mouth? What does he want of us? He wants to help us, they say. Yes, but among us he comes across as peculiarly at a loss. The conditions he lived in were so very different. Or does it in fact not have much to do with the circumstances – if he came in here, into my room, or visited me out in the factory, would everything immediately be changed, would all be well? Would my heart begin to pound and as it were move up a level and on towards him? My instinct tells me that he *cannot* come. That it would have no sense. Our world is a different one not just on the outside – it offers him no access. He would not *shine* through a ready-made coat, it is not true, he would not shine through. It is no coincidence that he went around in a seamless garment, and I believe that the core of light within him, what made him shine so strongly, day and night, has now long been dispersed and distributed differently. But that I think would be the least we could require of him if he was so great, that he somehow come out without remainder, yes, quite without remainder – leaving no trace ...

I cannot imagine that the *cross* was meant to *remain*, which after all was only a path, the way of the cross. Certainly it should not be imprinted on us everywhere as if with a branding-iron. It should be dispersed in him himself. For isn't it like *this*: he simply wanted to create a taller tree on which we could ripen the better. He, on the cross, is this new tree in God, and we were to be the fruits at the top of it, glad to be in the warm.

Now we should not always be talking about what went on before but, precisely, the *After* should have begun. This tree, it seems to me, should have become so one with us, or we with it, we *on* it, that we ought not always to be occupying ourselves with it but simply and calmly with God, to hold us up more purely in whom was after all its intention.

When I say God – it is a great conviction in me, not something I have learnt. The whole of creation, as it seems to me, says this word, without deliberation, though often out of deep thoughtfulness. If this man Christ has enabled

us to say it with a clearer voice, more roundly, more unas-
sailably, so much the better, but now let's leave him out of
it once and for all. We should not always be forced to fall
back into the toil and sorrow that it cost him to 'redeem'
us, as they put it. Let us finally come into this redemption.
– And in other ways too the Old Testament is full as it is
of forefingers pointing to God wherever one opens it, and
always if someone is weighed down he falls straight into
the middle of God. And once I tried to read the Koran. I
didn't get far, but this much I did understand: there is
another mighty forefinger, and if you follow it God stands
at the end in the midst of his eternal rising, in an orient
which will never be exhausted. Christ must have wanted
the same. To point. But the people here have been like
those dogs who don't understand pointing and think they
are meant to go for the hand. Instead of leaving Christ's
way of the cross, where the signpost was erected to reach
far into the night of sacrifice, instead of moving on from
this Via Crucis, Christianity has settled there and claims
to dwell in Christ there although there was no room in
him, not even for his mother, and not for Mary Magdalene
– as with anyone who points the way and is a gesture and
not a place to stay. – And for this reason they do not dwell
in Christ either, the stubborn at heart who are always re-
creating him and live from setting crosses which are
crooked or have been blown completely over upright
again. They have this press of people on their conscience,
this queuing up in an overcrowded place, they are to
blame that the journey does not continue in the direction
of the arms of the cross. They have made a *métier* of the
Christian purpose, a bourgeois occupation, *sur place*, a
pool that is alternately drained and then filled up again.

Everything that they do themselves, according to their own insuppressible natures (so far as they are still living beings), stands in contradiction to this curious disposition of theirs, and so they cloud their own waters and continually have to refresh them. They are so zealous they cannot stop making the Here and Now, which we should take pleasure and have trust in, base and worthless – and so more and more they deliver the earth into the hands of those who are prepared to turn it, the failed, suspect earth which is good for nothing better, to temporal, quick profit. This increasing ransacking of life, is it not a consequence of the devaluation of the Here and Now which has been going on for centuries? What madness, to divert us towards a beyond when we are surrounded by tasks and expectations and futures here. What deceit, to divest us of images of earthly delight in order to sell them to heaven behind our backs! Oh, it is high time the impoverished earth called in all the loans that have been made on her felicity to provide for a time that lies beyond the future. Does death really become more transparent by having these light-sources dragged behind it? And isn't everything that is taken away, given that no void can sustain itself, replaced by deceit and deception – are our cities filled with so much ugly artificial light and noise because true illumination and song have been surrendered to a Jerusalem which will only be entered later? Christ was perhaps right when, in a time of stale and threadbare gods, he spoke ill of the earthly; though (I cannot imagine it otherwise) it amounts to an insult directed at God not to see in what is granted and conceded to us here – so long as we use it correctly – something that fills us with happiness, completely and right to the outer margins of our senses! *To make the proper use of things, that's what it comes down to.* To take the Here and Now in one's hand, lovingly, with the heart, full of wonder, as, provisionally, the one thing we have: *that* is at once, to put it rather casually, the gist of God's great user's guide, *this* is what Saint Francis of Assisi meant to record in his hymn to the sun which as he lay dying he thought more splendid than the cross, whose only purpose in standing there was to *point towards* the sun. But what goes by the name of the Church had by then swollen into such a clamour of voices that the song of the dying man, drowned out in all quarters, was only caught by a few simple monks and infinitely assented to by the landscape of his lovely valley. How many such attempts there have been to produce a reconciliation between Christian denial and the manifest friendliness and good spirits of the earth. But elsewhere too, at the heart of the Church, even at its actual summit, the Here and Now managed to gain its plenitude and its native abundance. Why is the Church not praised for having been sturdy enough not to collapse under the living weight of certain popes, whose thrones were weighed down with bastards, courtesans and corpses? Did they not have more Christianity in them than the dry renovators of the Gospels – that is, Christianity that is living, irrepressible, transformed? What I mean is that we cannot know what will come of the great teachings, we just have to let them flow unabated and not take fright if they suddenly rush into the natural ravines of life and vanish underground and race along unknowable channels.

I once worked in Marseille for a few months. It was a special time for me, I owe it a great deal. Chance brought me together with a young painter who remained my friend until his death. He had a sickness of the lungs and was then just back from Tunis. We spent a lot of time together, and as the end of my employment coincided with his return to Paris, we were able to arrange things so as to stay a few days in Avignon. They are days I shall never forget. Partly because of the town itself, its buildings and environs, and also because during those days of uninterrupted and somehow heightened company my friend communicated to me many circumstances of, in particular, his *inner* life with that eloquence which, it seems, is peculiar to this kind of invalid at certain moments. All that he said had a curious clairvoyant force; through everything that rushed onwards in what were often almost breathless conversations, one could see so to speak the ground, the stones on the bottom ... I mean by that: more than just something of our own, nature itself, its oldest and hardest element, which after all we touch upon at so many points and on which we probably depend in our most driven moments, its gradient determining the way we incline. An unexpected and happy love affair also had a part in it, his heart was unusually exalted, for days on end, and as a result the changeful jet of his life shot up to a considerable height. To take in an extraordinary town and a more than pleasant landscape with someone in such a frame of mind is a rare privilege; and when I look back on those tender and at the same time passionate spring days, they appear to me as the only holiday I ever had in my life. The time was so laughably brief, to another it would have sufficed only for a few impressions; to me, not used to spending days of such freedom, it appeared vast. Yes, it almost seems wrong to go on calling *time* what was more nearly a new state of being free, truly felt as a *space*, a being-surrounded by openness, no passing or transience. I was catching up on my childhood then, if I can put it that way, and a part of my early youth, all that there had never been time to carry out in my life; I looked, I learned, I understood – and from those days also stems the experience that it is so easy for me, so truthful, so – as my friend would have expressed it – unproblematic, to say 'God'. How should this dwelling that the popes built for themselves there not strike me as colossal? I had the impression it could contain no interior space at all, but must be piled up of nothing but solid blocks of stone, as if the exiles had no other thought than to heap the weight of the papacy, its overweight, onto the scales of history. And this ecclesiastical palace really does tower up over the ancient torso of a Heracles statue which has been immured in the rocky foundations – 'Is it not', said Pierre, 'as if it had grown from this seed like a gigantic plant?' – That *this* should be Christianity, in one of its metamorphoses, would be much easier for me to under-stand than the idea that one might recognize its strength and its taste in the ever weaker brew of that *tisane* which, so it is claimed, is prepared from its first and most tender leaves.

For that spirit which people will have us believe is the authentic Christian one is not embodied in the cathedrals either. I could imagine that beneath some of them there rests the dislodged statue of a Greek goddess; so great a flowering, so much existence has shot up in them, even if, in a fear that first arose in that age, they strove away from that hidden body into the heavens, which the sound of their great bells was intended constantly to hold open.

After my return from Avignon I often went into churches, in the evenings and on Sundays, alone at first ... then later ...

I have a lover, almost a child still; she works at home, which when there is not much work often means that she finds herself in an awkward situation. She is skilful, she'd easily get a job in a factory, but she fears having a *patron*. Her conception of freedom is limitless. It will not surprise you that she also thinks of God as a kind of *patron*, even as the '*arch-patron*' as she told me, laughing, but with such fright in her eyes. It took a long time before she agreed to come with me one evening to St Eustache where I liked going for the music of the May devotions. Once we got as far as Maux together and had a look at gravestones in the church there. Gradually she noticed that God leaves you in peace in churches, that he demands nothing; you could think he wasn't there at all, *n'est-ce pas*, but then in the moment you are about to say something of the sort, said Marthe, that even in a church he doesn't exist, something holds you back. Perhaps only what over so many centuries people themselves have borne into this high, peculiarly fortified air. Or perhaps it is only that the resonance of the sweet and powerful music can never escape completely: yes, it must have penetrated into the stones long ago, and the stones must be strangely moved, these pillars and vaultings, and though stone is hard and difficult of access, even it is shaken in the end by the perpetual singing and these assaults from the organ, these onslaughts, these storms of hymns, every Sunday, these hurricanes on the great feast-days. The calm after a storm. That's what truly reigns in these old churches. I said so to Marthe. Windless calm. We listened, she got it at once, she has a wonderfully receptive nature. After that we sometimes went in, here and there, when we heard singing, and stood there, close together. Best of all was when we could see a stained-glass window, one of those old ones with many subjects and compartments, each one crammed with figures, big people and little towers and all sorts of goings-on. Nothing was thought to be unfit or too strange; there are castles and battles and a hunt, and the lovely white hart appears again and again amid the warm red and the burning blue. I was once given very old wine to drink. With these windows it is the same for the eyes, except that the wine was only dark red in my mouth – but here the same thing happens in blue and in violet and in green. *Everything* can be found in the old churches; there is no fear of anything, unlike in the new ones, where so to speak only good examples are present. Here there is also the bad and the wicked, the terrifying; the crippled, the destitute, what is ugly and unjust – and it is as if somehow it were all loved for God's sake. Here is the angel, who does not exist, and the devil, who does not exist; and man, who does exist, is in between them and, I cannot help it, their unreality makes him more real for me. In these places I can gather my thoughts and feelings about what it is to be human better than in the street, among people who have absolutely nothing recognizable about them. But that is a difficult thing to say. And what I now want to say is harder still to express. As far as the '*patron*', as far as power is concerned (this also gradually became clear to me in church, when we were completely taken up by the music), there is only *one* remedy against it: to go further than it does. Here is what I mean by this: in every power which claims some right over us we should always try to see all power, absolute power, power as such, the power of God. We should say to ourselves, there is only *one*, and understand power that is lesser, false, defective, as if it were that which takes hold of us legitimately. Would it not thus become harmless? If we always saw in every form of power, including the harmful and malicious, power itself – I mean that which ultimately has the right to be powerful – wouldn't we then overcome, intact as it were, the illegitimate and the arbitrary? Isn't our relationship to all the great unknown forces exactly like this? We experience none of them in their purity. We begin by accepting each with its shortcomings, which are perhaps commensurate with our own. – But isn't it the case with all scholars, explorers and inventors that the assumption that they were dealing with great forces suddenly led to the greatest of all? I am young, and there is much rebelliousness in me; – I cannot be certain that I act in accordance with my judgement in every case, where impatience and bitterness get the better of me; in my innermost being though, I know that subjection leads further than revolt. Subjection puts to shame any kind of usurpation, and in indescribable ways it contributes to the glorification of righteous power. The rebel strains to escape the attraction of a centre of power, and perhaps he will succeed in leaving this force-field; but once outside it he is in a void and has to look around for a new gravitation that will include him. And this usually has even less legitimacy than the first. So why not see at once, in the gravitation we find ourselves in, the supreme power, undeterred by its weaknesses and its fluctuations? Somewhere the arbitrary will come up against the law of its own accord, and we save energy if we leave it to convert itself. Admittedly this belongs to the lengthy, slow processes that stand in utter contradiction with the strange precipitations of our age. But alongside the most rapid movements there will always be slow ones, some indeed of such extreme slowness that we cannot sense their progress at all. But then that is what humanity is here for, is it not, to wait for what extends beyond the individual life. – From that perspective, the slow is often the most rapid of all, that is, it turns out that we only called it slow because is was something we could not measure.

And there exists, it seems to me, something utterly measureless, which people never tire of laying their hands on by means of standards, surveys, and institutions.

And it's here, in the love which, with their intolerable mixture of contempt, concupiscence and curiosity, they call 'sensual', that no doubt the worst effects of that debasement are to be sought which Christianity has seen fit to inflict on the earthly. Here everything is disfigurement and repression, although in fact we proceed from this most profound event and in turn possess in it the mid-point of our ecstasies. It is, if I may say so, harder and harder for me to comprehend how a doctrine which puts us in the wrong in the point where the whole of creation enjoys its most blessed right can with such steadfastness, if not actually prove its validity, nevertheless affirm it in all quarters.

Here too I am thinking of the intense conversations with my dead friend, vouchsafed me in the meadows of the Ile de la Barthelasse in the spring and later. On the very night before his death (he died the following afternoon shortly after five o'clock) he opened for me perspectives of such purity into a region of the blindest suffering that my life seemed to begin again in a thousand places and my voice, when I wanted to answer, deserted me. I did not know that there was such a thing as tears of joy. I wept my first, like a novice, into the hands of Pierre, who would be dead tomorrow, and felt the tide of life rise once more in him and overflow as these warm drops were added to it. Am I being excessive? What I am talking about *is* an excess, a too-muchness.

Let me ask you, Mr V., why, if they want to help us, we who are so often helpless, why do they fail us here, at the root of all experience? Whoever stood by us *there* could be assured that we would demand nothing further of him. For the succour he gave us there would grow of its own accord and would become greater and stronger at the same time as our life. And would never run out. Why are we not set at the heart of the most secret thing we have? Why do we have to creep around outside it and get in eventually like burglars and thieves, into our own beautiful sexuality, where we stray around and stumble and bump into one another and then rush out again, like people caught red-handed, into the shadowy light of Christianity? Why, if it is true that guilt and sin, because of the inner tension of our soul, had to be invented, why were they not fixed to another part of our bodies; why were they dropped in to wait until they dissolved in our pure well, poisoning and muddying it? Why has our sexuality been made homeless, instead of locating in it the celebration of our true abode?

Yes, I will admit that it is not right that it should belong to us, who are not capable of assuming and administering such an inexhaustible source of benediction. But why do we not belong to God from *this* point?

Church people would remind me that there is such a thing as marriage, though they would not be unaware of how matters stand with that institution. And it's no good moving the will to reproduction into the light of God's grace, my sexuality is not only directed towards my descendants, it is the mystery of my own life, and only because it cannot, as it seems, occupy a position at the centre of it have so many people pushed it to the edges of themselves and in doing so lost their equilibrium. What's to be done? The terrible untruth and uncertainty of our times has its cause in the inability to admit the happiness of sex, in this peculiarly misplaced culpability which is increasing all the time and divides us from the whole of the rest of nature and even from the child, although, as I learnt in that unforgettable night, the child's innocence does not at all consist as it were in being ignorant of sex – 'But', so Pierre said in an almost inaudible voice, 'that incomprehensible happiness which awakes in us in *one* place in the middle of the fruit-flesh of a close embrace is, in the child, still distributed anonymously over the whole body.' In order to describe the singular situation of our sensuality, one would have to be able to say: once we were children *everywhere*, now we only are in one place. – But if there is even a single person among us who is certain of this and capable of providing the evidence to show it, why do we look on while generation after generation comes to its senses and begins to stir under the rubble of Christian prejudices like someone left for dead in the dark, confined on all sides by sheer denial?

Mr V., I can't stop writing. I've been at it almost the whole night. I must sum up my thoughts. – Did I say that I am employed in a factory? I work in the office; sometimes

I'm also needed on the machines. Before that I once studied for a short while. Now, I just want to say what's on my mind. What I want, you see, is to be usable for God just as I am; what I do here, my work, I want to continue to do in his direction without my ray of light being refracted, if I may put it like that, not even in Christ, who was once the water for many. I cannot for example explain my machine to him, he cannot contain it. I know that you won't laugh if I put it so simply; it's best that way. God, on the other hand, I have the feeling that I can bring it to him, my machine and its first products, or even all my work; it goes into him without difficulty. As in the old days it was easy for shepherds to bring the gods of their lives a lamb or the fruits of the earth, the finest grapes.

You can see, Mr V., I have been able to write this long letter without once needing to use the word 'faith'. For that I think is an involved and difficult matter, and not for me. I will not let myself be worsened for Christ's sake, but want to be good for God. I do not want to be called a sinner from the outset, for perhaps I am not. I have mornings of such purity! I could talk with God, I need no one to help me draft letters to him.

Your poems I only know from that reading the other evening; I possess only a handful of books which mostly have to do with my job. I do have a few about art, and oddments of history, just what I was able to get hold of. – But your poems, you will have to accept this, have brought forth this commotion in me. My friend said once: Give us teachers who praise the Here and Now. You are such a one.

Notes

LETTERS TO A YOUNG POET

This edition presents the *Letters* as they were originally published in 1929, with Kappus's Preface. Franz Xaver Kappus, born in 1883 in Timişoara, died in Berlin in 1966. He was thus only eight years younger than Rilke.

Wiener Neustadt: A small town south of Vienna. Its Military Academy was the first of its kind in the world, founded in 1752 by Empress Maria Theresa.

Horaček: Rilke was taught by him from 1886 to 1890. As Kappus explains, Horaček was at that time chaplain in Sankt Pölten.

Sankt Pölten: The main city in Lower Austria.

Mährisch-Weisskirchen: The German name for the town of Hranice, in Moravia in the Czech Republic. It was then in the Austro-Hungarian Empire. Rilke was at the Military Academy there in 1890–91.

To Celebrate Myself: *Mir zur Feier*, a volume of poems, appeared in December 1899. It was Rilke's fifth published collection.

Paris, 17 February 1903

Rilke had been in Paris since the previous autumn. He had gone there to write a short book on the sculptor Auguste Rodin

(1840–1917), which he did very quickly (*Auguste Rodin*, finished in December 1902 and published in March 1903). Influenced by Rodin's working methods and personality, he had probably written 'The Panther', the earliest of the poems in the *Neue Gedichte* (*New Poems*), in November. There is not much trace of this new schooling in the sentiments of the letter.

p.5 *Leopardi*: The Italian poet Giacomo Leopardi (1798–1837).

p.8 *Professor Horaček*: See Kappus's Preface and the note.

Viareggio near Pisa (Italy), 5 April 1903

Rilke came to Viareggio to recover, not just physically, but artistically, from the demands laid on him by Rodin's example. He wanted both to find some response to the overwhelming experience of Paris and to return to the kind of inspiration-dependent writing that had served him well before. In a way he succeeded, writing the third and final part of the *Stunden-Buch* (*Book of Hours*), 'Das Buch von der Armut und vom Tode' ('The Book of Poverty and Death') from 13 to 20 April.

p.9 *in the past*: In spring 1898, when he began his lyrical drama *Die weisse Fürstin* (*The White Princess*).

p.10 *Jens Peter Jacobsen*: Jacobsen (1847–85) was an important influence on Rilke, as he always acknowledged, particularly on his novel, *The Notebooks of Malte Laurids Brigge*. The novel *Niels Lyhne* was published in 1880, 'Mogens' in 1872.

p.10 *Auguste Rodin*: See headnote to the letter from Paris, 17 February 1903. Rodin was the first really accomplished artist Rilke got to know well, and both work and person were of enduring importance to him, especially for the *New Poems* (1907/8), the second volume of which is dedicated 'A mon grand Ami Auguste Rodin'.

Viareggio near Pisa (Italy), 23 April 1903

p.12 *Marie Grubbe*: *Fru Marie Grubbe*, novel published in 1876.

p.13 *even if the translations are only moderate*: Rilke later translated a few Jacobsen poems himself.

p.13 *collected edition of Jacobsen's works*: This appeared in 1898–9; the translator was Marie Herzfeld.

p.13 *'Here roses should stand … '*: A German translation of this novella by Jacobsen appeared in a Berlin weekly in 1899, preceded by an essay by Gustav Gugitz to which Rilke is possibly referring.

p.14 *patience is all!*: The great lesson Rilke learnt from Rodin, as conveyed in a letter to Clara Rilke, his wife, on 5 September 1902: 'Il faut travailler, rien que travailler. Et il faut avoir patience' ('You have to work, just work. And you have to be patient').

p.14 *Richard Dehmel*: (1863–1920) Prominent poet at the time and quite important to Rilke a few years earlier. Kappus had asked what Rilke thought of him.

p.15–16 *my … books*: The estimate of '12 or 13' seems slightly generous. None of them contains the work for which Rilke is most admired today.

at present in Worpswede near Bremen, 16 July 1903

Worpswede is a small village in the plains of northern Germany which at the end of the nineteenth century became an artists' colony centred round Heinrich Vogeler, Otto Modersohn and Fritz Mackensen, but including more importantly Paula (Modersohn-) Becker. Rilke was there in 1900–1902 and met and married Clara Westhoff, a sculptor. They had a daughter on 12 December 1901. Rilke's book on four of the Worpswede artists had been published in February, just when the correspondence with Kappus began.

p.19 *'The desire to be a creator ... give form'*: Presumably, as a bit further on, a quotation from Kappus's letter.

p.22 *a profession*: Upon leaving the military academy, Kappus became a lieutenant.

Rome, 29 October 1903

From September 1903 to June 1904 Rilke was in Rome with his wife Clara.

p.24 *equestrian statue ... of Marcus Aurelius*: At the centre of the Capitol square. Marcus Aurelius's dates are 121–80. His is the only ancient equestrian statue to have survived.

p.24 *an old summer-house*: The Studio al Ponte in the park of the Strohl-Fern villa where Clara Rilke had already found a studio. Rilke moved in on 1 December.

p.25 *the book you announced in your letter*: *Im mohren-grauen Rock: Heiteres aus dem Leben der Zukünftigen*, by F.X.Kappus and E. von Torstenau (Vienna, 1903).

Rome, 23 December 1903

Rilke is now living in the grounds of the villa Strohl-Fern.

Rome, 14 May 1904

By this time, Rilke had written among other things the poem 'Orpheus. Eurydice. Hermes' and, in February, begun *The Notebooks of Malte Laurids Brigge*.

p.32 *we must hold fast to what is difficult*: Compare Yeats, 'the fascination of what's difficult'.

p.32 *'to hearken and to hammer day and night'*: Rilke uses almost this phrase near the beginning of his book on Rodin. Kappus had probably quoted it in his letter.

p.36 *especially in the northern countries*: Rilke is probably
thinking, among other things, of women writers like Edith
Nebelong and Karin Michaelis (both Danish), and Ellen Key
and Selma Lagerlöf (who were Swedish). Rilke knew Key
and Nebelong.

Borgeby gård, Flādie, Sweden, 12 August 1904

Rilke left Rome at the end of June and was in Sweden until the
beginning of December, a journey made under the auspices of
Ellen Key.

p.42 *the prisoners in Poe's tales*: Edgar Allan Poe (1809–49).
Rilke is probably thinking of 'The Pit and the Pendulum'
(first published 1842), in which a (single) prisoner attempts
to discover the dimensions of the dungeon he is in by feeling
his way along the walls.

Furuborg, Jonsered, Sweden, 4 November 1904

p.46 *a little work*: *Die Weise von Liebe und Tod des Cornets
Christoph Rilke* (*The Lay of the Love and Death of the
Cornet Christoph Rilke*) in its first published version. This text
of lyrical prose, concentrated as it is on a military character,
might have appealed to Kappus. Rilke wrote the first version
in 1899 and reworked it in August 1904 in Borgeby gård.

Paris, on the second day of Christmas 1908

More than four years separate this final letter from the last.
In the interim Rilke had travelled widely in Germany, Austria,
Flanders and Italy, but was mostly in Paris. The two volumes of
the *New Poems* appeared in 1907 and 1908.

p.48 *your solitary fort*: Kappus was stationed in Dalmatia, then
part of the Austro-Hungarian Empire.
p.48 *the noise of the sea*: The Adriatic.

THE LETTER FROM THE
YOUNG WORKER

This fictional letter was unpublished in Rilke's lifetime. It seems that it was written between 12 and 15 February 1922, in an interval between the completion of the tenth of the *Duino Elegies* and the composition of the fifth. Rilke had by then also written the first half of the *Sonnets to Orpheus* (at the beginning of the month) and would shortly write the second. The *Letter* was first published in 1933, together with a real letter addressed to Lotte Hepner, as *Über Gott: Zwei Briefe* (*On God: Two Letters*).

p.51 *Mr V.*: Some notes out of which the *Letter* seems to grow bear the title *Erinnerung an Verhaeren* (*Memories of Verhaeren*). Emile Verhaeren (1855–1916), the Belgian poet, had been an acquaintance of Rilke's since 1905 and was much admired by him.

p.52 *the way of the cross*: Rilke is punning here (and later) on the word 'Kreuzweg' whose usual sense is 'cross-roads' but which can also mean the Way of the Cross or the Stations of the Cross – the series of images representing the fourteen stages of Christ's Passion, or the events leading to the Crucifixion. Like the Latin *Via Crucis*, 'Kreuzweg' can also mean 'an extremely painful experience that has to be borne with fortitude' (*Oxford English Dictionary*), a sense Rilke also plays on.

p.53 *no room in him, not even for his mother*: See John 2:4.

p.53 *Mary Magdalene*: See Mark 16:9–11 and Luke 8:2. In Rilke's early, unpublished work *Christ: Eleven Visions* he has Jesus regret not having fathered a child with her.

p.53 *métier ... sur place*: 'Trade ... on the spot/fixed' (in French in the original).

p.54 *the Here and Now*: In German 'das Hiesige', an adjectival noun deriving from *hier*, here. Another possible translation would be 'the earthly' or 'the things of the earth'.

p.54 *a Jerusalem*: For the idea of a new Jerusalem, see Revelation 3:12 and Hebrews 12:22.

p.55 *Saint Francis of Assisi*: St Francis (1181–1226), whom Rilke had read about in a book by Paul Sabatier (*Vie de Saint François d'Assise*, 1894), appears at the end of the *Book of Hours*. He founded the Franciscan order ('a few simple monks') in 1209. His *Cantico del frate sole* was written two years before his death.

p.55 *certain popes*: Rilke is probably thinking of Renaissance popes like Sixtus IV or Innocent VIII whose reigns were famously corrupt and extravagant. Almost by accident, the worker is arguing, they were closer to God because closer to the exuberance of life than the 'renovators of the Gospels'.

p.57 *this dwelling that the popes built for themselves*: The Palais des Papes at Avignon. From 1309 to 1377 the popes were 'exiled' to Avignon, which became the papal seat.

p.57 *a Heracles statue*: The portal of the cathedral attached to the Palais des Papes is thought to be the remains of a temple to Heracles.

p.57 *tisane*: An infusion, often medicinal (in French in the original).

p.57 *in that age*: The time when the great Gothic cathedrals were built, roughly the twelfth to fifteenth centuries.

p.58 *a patron*: A boss (in French in the original).

p.58 *St Eustache*: A church in Paris on the rue Montmartre, still reputed for its music.

p.58 *the May devotions*: In honour of Mary.

p.58 *Maux*: Presumably Meaux, a cathedral town not far from Paris.

p.58–59 *Marthe … has a wonderfully receptive nature*: Rilke seems in this paragraph to be drawing on his own life. In 1911 he met Marthe Hennebert, a seventeen-year-old seamstress in difficult circumstances. In a letter of 14 January 1912 he wrote of her: 'everything flourishes in her into pure life, finds endless receptivity in her nature – it is a wonder'.

p.59 *Here is the angel, who does not exist*: Within a few days Rilke wrote a poem on the unicorn (one of the *Sonnets to Orpheus*) which begins 'O this is the beast that does not exist.'

p.61 *Ile de la Barthelasse*: An island on the Rhône near Avignon.

p.64 *Give us teachers who praise the Here and Now*: This was how Rilke now conceived of his own role, especially in the ninth *Duino Elegy* and in the *Sonnets to Orpheus*, all written at this time.

Afterword

Neither of the works translated here were published in Rilke's lifetime. Nor are they works in any very strict sense: the *Letters to a Young Poet* are ten letters written over an interval of nearly six years, not intended to be collected nor conceived as a whole; and *The Letter from the Young Worker* was jotted down quickly in pencil and never written out fair or apparently considered for publication. Yet the *Letters to a Young Poet*, since their appearance in 1929, have become Rilke's most widely read book, and the *Letter from the Young Worker*, though not so familiar, has long established itself as a key piece of his prose, setting out his thoughts with unflinching forcefulness. They come from opposite ends of Rilke's writing life. When he wrote his first letter to Franz Xaver Kappus, the 'young poet', in February 1903, Rilke had several collections behind him but had written hardly any of the work for which we read him nowadays. The fictive *Letter from the Young Worker* on the other hand was written nineteen years later in February 1922, the extraordinary February when he completed his *Duino Elegies* and wrote the *Sonnets to Orpheus* in what he called a 'nameless storm, a hurricane in the spirit'. So it belongs to Rilke's maturity, but as well as having preoccupations in common with the poems in whose company it arose, it connects to the letters to Kappus in ways that suggest that some of Rilke's ideas and concerns, and his basic attitude to life, didn't change very much.

Rilke was one of the great letter-writers. He wrote them every day, often many more than one, and really his letters, not all of which have been published, can be considered an integral part of his work, as he intimated himself. He often approached the never-quite-superable task of keeping his correspondence up to date as a way of getting into writing, a way of putting some-thing off and stealing up on it at the same time. The form of the letter, a text addressed to a specific person with no particular constraints, was clearly one which suited him. Quite extensive passages of his novel, *The Notebooks of Malte Laurids Brigge*, were originally written as letters to Lou Andreas-Salomé and to his wife Clara. And the fact that he used a fictitious letter to channel the preoccupations of the *Letter from the Young Worker* shows how instinctive the epistolary form became. Writing letters was Rilke's way of facing up to the world and locating himself in it, on a daily basis, and his poems were a more intense and more intricately ordered variation of the same process.

LETTERS TO A YOUNG POET

Franz Xaver Kappus, the recipient and editor of these letters, says in his own prefatory remarks virtually all that is needed by way of introduction to them. He had written to Rilke enclosing some of his own poems on learning that Rilke had once been, as he himself now was, a military cadet and that they even had a teacher in common. This was enough to make Kappus feel that Rilke would understand the dilemma of someone firmly set on a military career but finding that his literary interests were in conflict with it. (In fact Kappus managed a kind of compromise, though not one Rilke would have approved of, becoming a suc-cessful writer of popular fiction after having served and been wounded in the First World War.) For Kappus, Rilke seems pri-marily to have been the author of *To Celebrate Myself* (*Mir zur Feier*, 1899), which was the last volume of Rilke's poems to be written, with great virtuosity, in a largely derivative Art Nouveau style that was entirely of its time. Some sense of the kind of poetry this was can be gleaned from Kappus's own poem 'Sonnet', which Rilke returns to him, written out in his own hand, with his letter of 14 May 1904. Rilke's early poems were mostly better than this, but not dissimilar in mood and mode. But by the end of 1902, when he received Kappus's initial letter, Rilke had also published the *Book of Images* in its first edition, and written most of the *Book of Hours*, and these poems, though still not his major work, are already far more individual. In fact Kappus catches him on the point of becoming the Rilke we read Rilke for today: 'The Panther', perhaps the best known of the *New Poems*, Rilke's first incontrovertibly great book, seems to have been written in November 1902, and *Worpswede* and *Auguste Rodin*, the two books of art criticism which were important stepping-stones towards the syntactical subtleties and precise apprehensions of the *New Poems*, came out early in 1903. Rilke is coming into his own, and learning at an astonishing rate from the example of Rodin, whose working techniques and general way of being in the world he observed closely while writing his book on him.

Writing to Kappus, Rilke was also taking a sympathetic step back into an earlier stage of his career, so that much of what he says is actually at odds with his own practice at the time of writing and with the preoccupations dwelt on in letters to other correspondents written in the same period. It seems certain that Kappus's situation brought back strong memories of his own younger self and that, especially in the first few letters, he enters into a kind of complicity which draws on their similar experience as cadets and on Rilke's literary beginnings much more than on the insights he was rapidly finding his way to in Paris. One of the key words in the correspondence is 'deep' and its cognates. Rilke's repeated advice to Kappus is that he should delve down into his own self, that he should not look outwards

but within. 'Do not be distracted by surfaces,' he writes on 16
July 1903. Yet in Paris he had learned from Rodin precisely
the importance of surface as the locus of all that is knowable
about the world. One of the most striking things about the
Letters is that they are precisely calibrated to their recipient,
which has obviously not prevented them from having a much
wider appeal but does perhaps explain why that appeal is most
marked in the young.

To that extent Kappus's title *Letters to a Young Poet* is an
appropriate one, but in other ways it is misleading: Kappus sent
Rilke his poems and asked him whether they were any good,
but he also wrote a letter in which he opened his heart 'more
unreservedly than to anyone ever before' and it is this, more
than the verse, that Rilke responds to. Poetry, or even becoming
a poet, is only a small part of what they are concerned with.
The first three letters do contain some practical advice on writ-
ing, including a warning about irony and some suggestions for
reading (though what Rilke recommends is not verse but the
prose works of the Danish writer Jens Peter Jacobsen and the
Bible), but always it is advice that applies much more generally
than just to somebody wanting to become a poet. And this, of
course, is because for Rilke to be an artist was to live one's life
properly – the artistic and the existential were always insepa-
rable. Rilke is much more interested in Kappus the young man,
with his various difficulties and questions, than in Kappus the
young poet. His only response to the poems, beyond saying
that they have 'no identity of their own' (a comment which, he
must have been aware, applied equally well to his own early
verse) and that Kappus, not Rilke, must be the judge of their
validity, is to select the one he likes best (itself a useful service,
perhaps) and to send it back copied out in his own hand so that
Kappus can read it as if it were 'unknown' to him – a reminder
of times before the computer or even the typewriter.

During the period when most of the letters to Kappus were
written, Rilke was also writing in complete disarray to Lou

Andreas-Salomé, turning to her for advice much as Kappus had turned to him. It does seem to be the case that the apparent authority with which Rilke speaks to Kappus comes from a strong sense of how greatly in need he is of his own advice, and that the words are found because it is as much his own dilemmas as Kappus's that he is looking for answers to. Most of the time at least he doesn't dispense hard-won wisdom, but seems to be happening on the hidden structures that make up his existence, and he shares them as he finds them. Many of his thoughts have something improvised about them, such as when he is entertaining the difficult idea, in the letter of 12 August 1904, that the future 'comes upon us' much sooner than is actually apparent, and that we are in effect always struggling to catch up with things that have already, unknown to us, occurred. In trying to look at life not as it seems, Rilke is acting according to his own precept of 'solitude', attending to the world as if for the first time.

THE LETTER FROM THE YOUNG WORKER

On the face of it, although the 'worker' is writing out of a state of 'commotion', the *Letter from the Young Worker* is marked by greater certainty. Its tone is firm and clear, and Rilke is not so much discovering truths as finding the best expression for beliefs he had held from very early on. The *Letter* is a polemic against Christianity, and Rilke had begun this in one of his earliest works, *Christ: Eleven Visions* (written 1896–8), a sequence of poems he never published, in which he has Christ, in various guises, travel through the world that is his legacy, full of remorse for what his teachings have wrought. The *Letter* takes the form of an address to 'Mr V.', which the manuscript makes clear refers to Emile Verhaeren, the Belgian poet whom Rilke got to know in Paris in 1905 and whom he always held in high regard. Verhaeren had died falling under

a train in 1916, and Rilke read and reread his work in the
following years, especially the posthumous collection *Les
Flammes hautes* (1917). In the manuscript, the *Letter from the
Young Worker* is preceded by the crossed-out words 'If I were
a young worker I should have written you something like this.'
It is a letter to a dead friend, a kind of homage to Verhaeren,
whom the worker holds up as a 'teacher who praises the Here
and Now'. He thus sets poetry, which heightens our awareness
of the beauty and value of the world we live in, against Chris-
tianity, which according to the *Letter* has damaged life and
exploited it, diminishing the pleasure we take in the present
in favour of the idea of an afterlife: 'What deceit, to divest us
of images of earthly delight in order to sell them to heaven
behind our backs!'

Rilke wrote the *Letter* while in the middle of his great late
works, the *Duino Elegies* and the *Sonnets to Orpheus*, both
of which can be said to dedicate themselves to the earth. It
was written in the pad that also contains drafts of the Tenth
Elegy at the beginning and of the Fifth (the last to be written)
at the end, and Rilke had by then completed the first part of
the *Sonnets to Orpheus* and would shortly write the second.
The validation of poetry it contains can be understood as a
self-validation, and Rilke's Orpheus is indeed in many ways a
counter-figure to Christ, focusing on the 'earthly' and the 'Here
and Now', words which are common to both the *Letter* and
the *Sonnets to Orpheus*. That the *Letter* emerged from such a
context, when anyone might have thought that Rilke was taken
up with other things, points to the charge of necessity it carries,
and this quality is audible in its every sentence, a hard, clear,
uncompromising quality which does not eschew the colloquial
or the direct but uses whatever means channel its energy best.
'A work of art is good if it has arisen out of necessity,' Rilke
had written to Kappus in his first letter to him, and this one evi-
dently did. Despite this he made no mention of the text in his
correspondence.

Rilke seems to adopt the persona of the worker as a way of emphasizing that he is speaking out of the present, the 'machine age' (the worker is a factory-worker who spends most of his time behind a desk and is only rarely on the machines, but this doesn't prevent him from referring to 'my machine'). There is a comparable attention to modernity, to the machine and to technological advances like aeroplane flight, in some of the *Sonnets to Orpheus*. The worker's first objection to Christ is that he belongs to another era: 'The conditions he lived in were so very different.' He wore a seamless garment whereas now clothes are bought off the peg, one size fits all. The worker/Rilke does not doubt the 'core of light' that dwelled in him, just as he does not want to do without God (the *Letter* is not anti-religious), but he thinks the time in which Christ was necessary is long over and that having served his purpose of bodying forth God he should have vanished, 'without remainder'. Instead, he has become the focal point of a religion and has left the very palpable trace of the crucifix.

The ubiquity of the cross is something that Rilke regards as a misunderstanding: it was meant as a pointer beyond itself, to God, but has ended up getting in the way. Rilke begins a play on words here whose ramifications run outwards to other of his works in a kind of secret tracery that relates the *Letter*'s main preoccupations. He says that the cross was only a crossroads (a point to move on from rather than a destination), where the German word *Kreuzweg* means Way of the Cross as well as crossroads. *Kreuzweg* was a word Rilke was fond of, and it seems to have almost a private meaning for him. This is first intimated in a sentence from his book on Rodin: 'The person who rises at night and softly goes to another is like a digger for treasure who wants to excavate the great and necessary happiness that lies at the crossroads of [the] sex.' It is then reprised in an erotic poem of 1915: 'Raised by you the god's form stands / at the gentle crossroads beneath my clothes.' The 'gentle crossroads' in these lines is the crotch, and instead of a cross there stands a phallic god, which the poem also refers to as a Herma. The *Kreuzweg* is not only a place of suffering, a *Via Crucis*, but a place of pleasure.

The *Letter* as a whole envisages the displacement of the Christian mystery by the sexual mystery, of the cross by the genitals, and it culminates in the words 'But why do we not belong to God from *this* point?' Like D. H. Lawrence, a convergence with whose views he noted when reading a translation of the essay 'On being religious' in 1924, Rilke imagines (longs for) a variety of religious experience in which we are not estranged from what in the letter to Kappus of 16 July 1903 he calls our 'best possession'. In a letter written the month after the *Letter from the Young Worker* he even follows this thought with the idea that such a religion might inaugurate a return of the ancient gods, in a characteristically Rilkean inversion of the notion that Christ was the last of them:

> The terrible thing is that we possess no religion in which these experiences, literal and tangible as they are (for, at the same time, so unutterable and so untouchable), may be raised into God, into the protection of a phallic deity, a deity that will perhaps be the *first* with which a company of gods might come over humankind again after so long an absence.
>
> (to Rudolf Bodländer, 23 March 1922)

The word *Kreuzweg* is also used in the last of the *Sonnets to Orpheus*, in the phrase 'the crossroads of your senses' (addressed to Orpheus). At this point where the senses cross, the poem says, 'sense' (meaning) occurs. The 'secret' meaning of *Kreuzweg* (an open secret in the end) allows us to understand the crotch as a kind of sensorium, a percipient centre, and to see sexuality as partaking in all five usual senses as a vital element in our apprehension of the earthly. Orpheus becomes implicitly a sexual god (Rilke refers to him as a god rather than a demigod), and the *Sonnets* thus connect sexuality and poetry much as the *Letter from the Young Worker* does. This is all in keeping with insights first articulated in the *Letters to a Young Poet*. There Rilke had called sexual desire 'a way of knowing the world', and had seen artistic and sexual experience as phenomena which were 'really just different forms of one and the same desire and felicity'.

Charlie Louth 2011

Translator's Note and Further Reading

The *Letters to a Young Poet* have been translated many times before, but that is one mark of their importance. In part to justify a new translation, I have tried to keep pretty close to Rilke's actual wording, tracing in some degree his syntax and rhythms, and even keeping much of his eccentric punctuation. Since most of Rilke's language in these letters is marked by a great ease, it could well be that I have distanced myself from the *Letters'* original habitat. Another recent translation, Stephen Cohn's, takes a very nearly opposite course, and recasts the German into wholly new English sentences which sometimes bear little relation to the way Rilke is saying something; though of course, since its words feel easy and at home, it could be argued that they are in fact very close to Rilke's. No one translation will ever do in the end. For the *Letter from the Young Worker* it seemed even more important to cleave to the form of the original, as the shifts in tone, the switches in and out of the colloquial and the often abrupt and unusual way of putting things are essential to the kind of text it is.

Stephen Cohn's versions of *Letters to a Young Poet* are available in Rainer Maria Rilke, *The Sonnets to Orpheus with Letters to a Young Poet*, tr. Stephen Cohn (Carcanet, 2000). As suggested in the Afterword, the *Sonnets to Orpheus* and the *Letter from the Young Worker* are closely related, and anyone wanting to read the *Sonnets* in English should probably turn to: Don Paterson, *Orpheus: A Version of Rilke's* Die Sonette an Orpheus (Faber, 2006). Rilke's correspondence can best be pursued in English by reading Rainer Maria Rilke and Lou Andreas-Salomé, *The Correspondence*, tr. Edward Snow and Michael Winkler (Norton, 2006). Anyone wanting to find out more about Rilke's life has a choice between two large biographies: Donald Prater, *A Ringing Glass: The Life of Rainer Maria Rilke* (Oxford University Press, 1986), and Ralph Freedman, *Life of a Poet: Rainer Maria Rilke* (Farrar, Straus and Giroux, 1996); also useful is *The Cambridge Companion to Rainer Maria Rilke*, ed. Karen Leeder and Robert Vilain (Cambridge University Press, 2010).

I should like to thank Monica Schmoller again for her excellent copy-editing.

Charlie Louth 2011